WESTERN ICELANDIC SHORT

Translated by
Kirsten Wolf and Árný Hjaltadóttir

WESTERN ICELANDIC
SHORT STORIES

University of Manitoba Press

© The University of Manitoba Press 1992
Winnipeg, Canada R3T 2N2
Printed in Canada
Printed on acid-free paper ∞

Design: Norman Schmidt

The publication of this volume was assisted by the Canada
Council/Conseil des Arts du Canada and by the Manitoba Arts
Council/Conseil des Arts du Manitoba.

Cataloguing in Publication Data

Main entry under title:
Western Icelandic short stories

Translation of 12 Icelandic-Canadian stories originally published
individually between 1895 and 1930.
Includes bibliographical references.
ISBN 0-88755-628-0

1. Short stories, Canadian (Icelandic)*
I. Wolf, Kirsten, 1959-   II. Árný Hjaltadóttir, 1950-

PS8331.I23W4 1991   C839'.693' 01   C91-097195-1

CONTENTS

INTRODUCTION

THE EMIGRATION OF ICELANDERS to North America was part of a more general movement taking place in Europe during the eighteenth and nineteenth centuries, and as such the Icelanders were but following the example of their Scandinavian neighbours.[1] More directly, perhaps, the emigration was a result of political dissatisfaction and unfavourable economic conditions caused among other things by an epidemic that carried off 200,000 sheep in the years between 1856 and 1860, the extraordinarily hard winter of 1858-1859, and the eruption of Dyngjufjöll in 1875, which covered large areas in the north and east of Iceland with volcanic ash, and drove many people from their homes.

The year 1870 is generally considered the year the emigration to North America began, when four Icelanders left for Washington Island, on Lake Michigan, in Wisconsin. (This is discounting a score of Icelandic converts to the Mormon religion, who left for Utah in the period between 1855 and 1871, settling in the Spanish Fork district.) More Icelanders joined the group in 1871, and new settlers then began to arrive with increasing steadiness. In 1872, twenty-two Icelanders left for North America; the group included two young men, Páll Þorláksson (1849-1882), who headed a group that settled in Milwaukee, Wisconsin, and Sigtryggur Jónasson (1852-1942), who left Iceland alone and went to Ontario. Both were to become instrumental in the emigration movement and are commonly referred to as the "fathers of Icelandic settlement" in North America, the former in the United States and the latter in Canada.

Letters to Iceland from Páll Þorláksson and Sigtryggur Jónasson in the autumn and winter of 1872-1873 encouraged Icelanders to emigrate to North America. In 1873, a group of approximately 165 Icelanders left Iceland, and in 1874, another group of roughly 365 Icelanders arrived in North America. The Icelanders spread from one coast to the other, but the major centres of settlement were, at least during the first years, Wisconsin (Washington Island and Milwaukee), North Dakota, Ontario (Rosseau in the Muskoka area and Kinmount), and Nova Scotia (the Mooseland Heights). A number of these initial settlements proved unsuitable, however, and were later largely abandoned.

An active search for a colony site within which all the Icelandic immigrants could settle began in 1874. Ontario was considered a suitable place for settlement, but by 1875 it had become apparent that there was no territory in the Free Grant area appropriate for a large Icelandic colony. It was then decided to explore the west, especially the Red River Valley. A party of six, including Sigtryggur Jónasson, made an expedition to investigate the area, and were favourably impressed. The territory selected for the colony site extended 36 miles along the west shore of Lake Winnipeg about ten miles in depth, commencing at the boundary of the province of Manitoba on the south (Boundary Creek at Winnipeg Beach) and extending north of the White Mud River (later Icelandic River) including Big Island. They named the region New Iceland (Nýja Ísland), and the order-in-council setting out the reserve was issued that same year. Thus an entirely Icelandic state was founded with a separate constitution that existed for ten years (1877-1887). This area north of the Province of Manitoba was at that time a part of the North-West Territories, but was included in the District of Keewatin when that district was formed in 1876. Precisely why the government of the new nation of Canada was willing to give such freedom to a population from a small island nation in the North Atlantic must be left to speculation, although it may well be that the government sought to open up the western frontier and thus used whatever means available to bring new settlers to those regions of what was later to become part of Canada.

Government aid to finance the move was secured, and a group of approximately 280 Icelanders from Ontario and Wisconsin arrived in Winnipeg in the autumn of 1875, headed by John Taylor (1812-

1884), who from the outset had been helpful to the Icelandic immigrants and who had been appointed Icelandic agent by the Dominion Government. From Winnipeg, they proceeded to Willow Point, where they settled and established themselves in what is now Gimli, the first Icelandic town in North America. Some 1,200 to 1,400 Icelanders arrived in Canada in 1876, and, apart from a few who went to Nova Scotia, they all proceeded to New Iceland. But the hardships that faced the colonists in New Iceland, especially the smallpox epidemic of 1876-1877, which killed over 100 Icelandic settlers, the great flood of 1879, and, not least, the religious controversy between Reverend Jón Bjarnason (1845-1914), one of the leaders of the orthodox church in America, and the fundamentalist preacher Reverend Páll Þorláksson, which began in 1877-1878 and which practically divided the colony into two factions, the "Jón's men" and the "Páll's men," caused many of the immigrants to leave New Iceland. Several settlers, in particular Páll Þorláksson's followers, left for North Dakota (Pembina County) in 1878-1879. Others left for "the Argyle settlement," Manitoba, in 1881, where they successfully formed a new community that grew rapidly; in 1890, there were some 700 Icelandic people in this new district. New Iceland eventually lost its status and influence as the leading Icelandic settlement, and by the end of 1881 three-quarters of the population of New Iceland had left, leaving only 250. Immigration into the colony was resumed in 1883 and resulted in increased trade, a renewal of religious activity, and the re-establishment of schools. Despite this growth, the centre of Icelandic settlement had by then been transferred to Winnipeg, which has come to be known as the capital of the Icelanders in the West. The site selected was south of Broadway, not far from the junction of the Red and Assiniboine rivers, known as the Hudson's Bay Flats, a district commonly called Shanty Town. From then on, the pattern of immigration changed, with no one area becoming the focal point.

The result was that many smaller Icelandic settlements were formed in Manitoba, in what was then the North-West Territories, and in the United States, especially the mid-western states. Icelandic settlement in Saskatchewan, in the districts of Þingvalla, Lögberg, Hólar (later Tantallon), and Foam Lake, thus began in 1885, primarily by settlers who had come directly from Iceland and who only just paused in Winnipeg. However, in the second period of settlement, the so-called Lakes Settlement, which commenced at the turn of the century, the settlers who moved in had resided for some years in other Icelandic settlements. Similarly, the Tindastóll (later Markerville) settlement in Alberta was formed not by new immigrants but by a group of Icelanders who in 1888-1889 left Pembina County, North Dakota. Other Icelandic settlers later left for Calgary, and after the turn of the century some moved to Edmonton. Finally, a number of Icelandic settlers moved to British Columbia (Victoria); the move westward began in the mid-1880s, and although many left Victoria for Point Roberts, Washington, in 1894, there has always been a fairly large settlement of Icelanders in Victoria. Settlement in Vancouver began somewhat later and was slow and irregular since most of the settlers came singly or in single families. In fact, there is only one documented case of a group arriving with the intention of setting up an Icelandic district in the province; this group intended to form a community on the Queen Charlotte Islands, but was diverted to what became the Osland Settlement.

The emigration of Icelanders to North America caused an explosion of literary creativity. Ólafur F. Hjartar's bibliography, *Vesturheimsprent,*[2] attests to this unusual literary activity during the early stage in the growth of Western Icelandic (or Icelandic-Canadian literature, as it is commonly designated) and reveals the existence of a thriving literary circle that included known authors and amateur enthusiasts alike. But many more authors can be added to Ólafur F. Hjartar's list, authors whose works appear in a variety of Western Icelandic newspapers, magazines and journals from this early period, such as *Framfari* (1877-1880), the first Western Icelandic newspaper, which was later followed by *Leifur* (1883-1886), and the weeklies *Heimskringla* (1886›) and *Lögberg* (1888›). There were also several "church-journals," such as *Heimir* (1904-1914), associated with the Unitarian Church, and *Sameiningin* (1886-1964), *Aldamót* (1891-1903), and *Áramót* (1905-1909), all associated with the Evangelical-Lutheran Church. Other publications include *Freyja* (1898-1910), *Vínland* (1902-1908), *Breiðablik* (1906-1914), *Tímarit Þjóðræknisfélags Íslendinga* (1919-1969) and *Saga* (1925-1931) to mention but a few.

But literary expression also found ready support through a network of reading circles and cultural and literary societies, such as "Hið íslenzka menningarfélag" ("The Icelandic Cultural Society"), founded in North Dakota in 1888, "Hagyrðingafélagið" ("The Verse Maker's Club"), founded in Winnipeg in 1903, and "Þjóðræknisfélag Íslendinga í Vesturheimi" ("The Icelandic National League in America"), founded in 1919. These societies, newspapers and magazines were as much a product of the literary activity as they were factors that promoted it.

The earliest phase of Western Icelandic writings in many respects presents itself as an imported literature: its practitioners carried with them the Icelandic training of an older generation, reflecting the prevailing tastes and customs of their earlier years in Iceland. The literature thus also bears a strong imprint of national romanticism as it blends the virtues of the old heroic Saga Age with the love of the homeland and the beauty of the native tongue. Yet Western Icelandic literature remains distinct from its literary ancestor in that it reflects as well the varying themes and cultural and literary trends of its new environment, sometimes uneasily yoked to its literary heritage, at other times – and with varying success – yielding a new brand of writing strongly marked by an awareness of the two cultural streams of Iceland and of a newly adopted country.

The national romantic movement in Iceland received its most focused literary expression through poetry, primarily through the lyric, and, as to be expected, the literary form chiefly cultivated by the Western Icelanders was in turn poetry. Here we find not only a large measure of nostalgic poems dedicated to the homeland the immigrants had been compelled to leave, tributes and odes to the adopted country, and nature poems about the Rocky Mountains, the Alberta foothills, the prairies, Lake Winnipeg, and the seasons, but also a large quantity of occasional verse, memorial and laudatory poems, nuptial and wedding-anniversary odes, epigrams and the like. Prose was also being written during this period, however, and spans a broad spectrum of genres. Apart from essays, articles and lectures, we find novels and short stories, memoirs and plays. Whereas poetry featured Icelandic themes to a very considerable extent, prose writing was largely, though not exclusively, North American in subject matter, and portrayed life among Icelanders in North America, especially in the Icelandic settlements in Manitoba and Nova Scotia.

The present collection of Western Icelandic short stories offers a representative selection of works written originally in Icelandic by twelve prose fiction writers during the period from approximately 1895 to 1930. A number of the authors included in this volume are, however, also known for their poetry – notably Stephan G. Stephansson, but also Guðrún H. Finnsdóttir, Jóhann Magnús Bjarnason, and Þorsteinn Þ. Þorsteinsson. Except for Arnrún frá Felli's "Stones for Bread," which is set in Iceland, and the sketches in Stephan G. Stephansson's "Motes in a Sun-Beam," which are difficult to locate geographically, all the stories are set in North America, the majority in New Iceland or Winnipeg.

Judged by modern literary standards, the stories in this collection are somewhat uneven in their quality. Some, like Bergþór E. Johnson's "The Sentence," strike the reader as laboured, even juvenile. Its imagery is forced, its metaphors uninspired, and its theme, the conflicting obligations to family and country, less than poignantly illustrated. As in "The Sentence," the characters of Friðrik J. Bergmann's "Fellow Students," lack developed voices, and a sense of control over the narrative is wanting. In both stories the characters are flat, one-dimensional figures struggling for definition. Þorsteinn Þ. Þorsteinsson's "In Days of Yore," although superior to "The Sentence" and "Fellow Students," is overloaded with detail. Such works, however, are entirely characteristic of their authors, and, even if they are less than exemplary in their literary efforts, they allow us to form a picture of the range of literary activity among first- and second-generation Western Icelandic writers.

But we see as well among these early authors some of the best writers the period has to offer. It is to Stephan G. Stephansson that a place of honour is to be accorded. His finely crafted prose, his mastery of voice and imagery, his controlled sense of narrative movement yield at once something mysteriously beautiful and profound in his writings:

> The daylight was murky, like nightfall. The calm, cold weather trailed over the mouth of the valley and over the slopes.

Due south the clouds broke, showing the rayless sun, which looked phosphorescent in the dusky pine forest; yet it seemed so near, as if it were hanging between the glacier and the bottom of the valley. Closer, in the deepest part of the valley, two light, golden shields glittered at the bottom of the grey snow coffin. There the river spread out along the flat sand banks, and the sun had stolen down there somehow, like the beautiful memories from one's youth.

Guðrún H. Finnsdóttir, whose writings find strength and depth in careful attention to detail, likewise earns a place of prominence among Western Icelandic writers. Here is her description of a Manitoba winter:

It was Manitoba Christmas weather; a clear, starspangled sky, bright moonlight and a motionless calm. The evening was so still and silent; it was as if the night held its breath. There was severe frost, and silvery-white, hard-frozen snow covered everything and rose in waves and crests like a stiffened ocean. Indeed, like the ocean, the prairie in many ways fills the souls of men with a burning desire to wander off to explore endless dimensions. In summer it brings on melancholy, but in winter fear and despair, for when the prairie is covered with snow, it is even more terrible than the ocean, because its tranquility and desolation is even greater. One feels as if death is on the look-out behind every mound of snow. But this time the snow-covered prairie was only a magic place they flew over. The soft snow whirled beneath the horse's hooves and crunched under the runners on the sled. The air, crisp and cold, burned and stung their faces, and with each breath the frost grabbed their nostrils with its hairy paws.

The diversity of styles and themes among these stories can be seen as well, by comparison, in Gunnsteinn Eyjólfsson's "How I Defeated the Local Board," about do-little Jón of Strympa's adventures in New Iceland; it is a meandering account, yet not without a narrative structure. The main character's guiding advice, "own nothing and do nothing," opens the way to a lively display of Gunnsteinn Eyjólfsson's satiric wit and comic touches, as in his description of Jón's wife Ásdís, who also bears the same name as Jón's cow. The result is delightful, comic confusion:

> I mentioned earlier that my wife's name is Ásdís. She's three years older than I am and a very talented and respectable woman. She's the stepdaughter of Þorsteinn, who lived at Yxnaþúfa for a long time – a man of honour and a good farmer. I'm surprised that *Sunnanfari* never had a picture of him because he had a superior cow that gave milk every year. My Ásdís was the eldest of the sisters. She was of Danish descent, the offspring of an outstanding bull, and all the farmers in the district competed for the heifers she dropped. I never knew how it came about that Ásdís and I went to America.

More satirical is Kveldúlfur's "Hávarður from Krókur," which, in its dual perspective on the death of Hávarður (his own and his fellow politicians'), pointedly attacks the hypocrisy and self-centredness of those entrenched in the mire of politics.

Religion and the Bible also inform a number of the stories in this collection. Biblical allusion provides the inspiration for Arnrún frá Felli's bittersweet story "Stones for Bread," and Grímur Grímsson's "Greater Love Hath No Man than This . . . ," as its title announces, takes as its point of departure a passage from John 15:13: "Greater love hath no man than this, that a man lay down his life for his friends." An instance of extreme self-sacrifice forms the core of this story, as Líndal willingly ends his hopes for a career and for the hand of the woman he loves for the sake of advancing his friend and fellow-student Frímann. Intentionally or not on the author's part, the story raises the question of whether such sacrifice is ultimately praiseworthy. Religion also informs Stephan G. Stephansson's "The Death of Old Guðmundur the Student," but, unlike the other stories, it provides a forum for critical discussion.

But it is to Old Norse-Icelandic literature, the Sagas of Icelanders and the Eddas, that a number of the stories contained in this volume owe their most obvious debt. Jóhann Magnús Bjarnason's description of the protagonist Hrómundur in his folktale-like story "An Icelandic

Giant" differs little from the full-length portrait given of Egill Skalla-Grímsson in *Egils saga:*

> He did not seem very tall when he was standing by himself, but he was nonetheless a good six feet tall. So stocky was he around his shoulders and body that his stoutness made him seem smaller. I saw him among Scotsmen who were taller than him, but no one was as thick-set and strong-looking. I saw him also among Irishmen, who appeared stouter than him, but that was because they were fatter and not as round, and he was always a big-boned man. I have seen bigger shoulders than his, but never a broader back, and no one with thicker arms nor more broad-chested. His neck was enormously thick, and for that reason his shoulders did not seem as broad. All his joints were large, and the muscles on his arms and legs were exceedingly big, compact, and as hard as stone. His hands were not big in the same way, but they were thick and strong and with continuous small scars and cracks, which showed that they had not been idle in his life.
>
> His face was far from handsome. His forehead was low and covered with numerous wrinkles. His eyebrows were hairy, heavy and big, almost terrifying. His jaws were long and strong. His nose was rather thin and high and not well-shaped. But his eyes showed that he was of Norse descent. They were blue – sky-blue – hard, cold and piercing. It is said that men who have such eyes are usually dutiful sons, good husbands, the best of fathers, friends to their friends, and faithful. On the other hand, they are always unwieldy and moody when something wrong is done to them, and then they do not spare anyone. Hrómundur had fair hair, a little curly at the back. On his cheeks and chin he had a big, fair and almost invisible beard, which was seldom combed or taken care of. And when he was silent, he pressed his lips together; it is said that this is an unfailing sign of discreetness and firmness.

Indeed, the narrator compares him with the chief characters in the Sagas of Icelanders and says, "When I was a boy and read the old Icelandic sagas, I often thought about him. I did not find him similar to Gunnar or Grettir or Skarphéðinn, but I often thought that Egill

Skalla-Grímsson was like him, not because of Egill's wisdom and enterprise, but rather because of the vigour, the temper, and the supernatural strength that they had in common." Jóhannes P. Pálsson, in his short story "Álfur of Borg," draws not only his theme and portrayal of the protagonist Álfur from saga literature, but also to a very large extent structures his story in a manner similar to a particular medieval Icelandic literary genre, the short embedded narratives, so-called *þættir* (sing. *þáttr*). Indeed, the story shows a number of affinities with the popular *Auðunar þáttr vestfirzka* ("The Tale of Auðunn of the West Fjords").[3] Stephan G. Stephansson's sketch "Greybeard," about the anonymous guest in King Útsteinn's tent, in some respects echoes *Norna-Gests þáttr* ("The Tale of Norna-Gestr") and the eddic poem *Hárbarðsljóð* ("The Lay of Hárbarðr [i.e., Greybeard=Odin]") as it combines question-and-answer with the motif of the mysterious and all-wise traveller who, through his life story, imparts wisdom to all who are willing to hear his words.

The stories contained in this collection stand, above all, as literary artifacts, revealing the literary tastes and influences of these early writers and their audiences as well as their ethnic heritage as Western Icelanders. In all, they bear witness to the vibrant literary activity among Western Icelanders at the turn of the nineteenth century and continuing into the early decades of the twentieth century, the result of which was the emergence of a literature that bears a unique cultural imprint.

In rendering the stories into English, we have kept as close as possible to the originals in an attempt to capture their individual styles and modes of expression, though without doing actual violence to English usage. We have retained Icelandic spelling of proper names throughout and, in order to keep the Icelandic flavour of the stories, have refrained from normalizing the Icelandic characters ð (the *th*-sound as in "bathe") and þ (the *th*-sound as in "bath"), the accented vowels á (as in "house"), é (roughly as in "yes"), í (as in "sleet"), ó (as in "those"), ú (roughly as in "lose"), ý (as in "feet"), and the mutated vowels æ (roughly as in "five") and ö (roughly as in "burn").

For patient and imaginative help, especially with the verses in this translation, we are grateful to Julian Meldon D'Arcy of the University of Iceland, who also read through the entire manuscript and made many improvements. We are indebted, too, to Phillip Pulsiano of Villanova University for his correction of our initial efforts and critical comments on the introduction, to Sigrid Johnson, head of the Icelandic Collection at the University of Manitoba, and her assistant, Kristrun Turner, for their assistance in obtaining biographical information on the various Western Icelandic writers, and to P.M. Mitchell, curator of the Fiske Icelandic Collection at Cornell University, for his help in locating rare works. We are grateful also to Lionel Levesque and Elaine Hall, both of Winnipeg, Paul Sigurdson of Morden, and Daniel Doucette of Grosse Isle for many useful suggestions.

We wish to thank the Icelandic Language and Literature Fund at the University of Manitoba for financial assistance for this project and the staff of the University of Manitoba Press for their smooth handling of the book throughout its production.

Kirsten Wolf
Winnipeg 1991

NOTES

[1] In the following, I rely on Thorstína Jackson, *Saga Íslendinga í Norður-Dakota* (Winnipeg, 1926, rpt. Reykjavík, 1982); Þorsteinn Þ. Þorsteinsson and Tryggvi J. Olesen, *Saga Íslendinga í Vesturheimi,* 5 vols. (Winnipeg and Reykjavík, 1940-1953); Wilhelm Kristjanson, *The Icelandic People in Manitoba: A Manitoba Saga* (Winnipeg, 1965, rpt. 1990); W. J. Lindal, *The Icelanders in Canada,* Canada Ethnica 2 (Winnipeg, 1967); James M. Richtik, "Chain Migration Among Icelandic Settlers in Canada to 1891," in Gurli Aagaard Woods, ed., *Scandinavian-Canadian Studies* 2 (1986), pp. 73-88; John S. Matthiasson, "Adaptation to an Ethnic Structure: The Urban Icelandic-Canadians of Winnipeg," in E. Paul Durrenberger and Gísli Pálsson, eds., *The Anthropology of Iceland* (Iowa City, 1989), pp. 157-175.

[2] Ólafur F. Hjartar, *Vesturheimsprent. Skrá um rit á íslensku prentuð vestan hafs og austan af Vestur-Íslendingum eða varðandi þá. A bibliography of publications in Icelandic printed in North America or elsewhere by or relating to the Icelandic settlers in the West (*Reykjavík, 1986).

[3] Cf. Kirsten Wolf, "Jóhannes P. Pálsson's *Álfur of Borg* and Medieval Icelandic *þættir," The Icelandic Canadian* 49:4 (1991), pp. 35-41.

WESTERN ICELANDIC SHORT STORIES

STONES FOR BREAD

Arnrún frá Felli

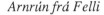

Arnrún frá Felli (pen name for Guðrún Tómasdóttir, also known as Mrs. Charles F. Bjarnason,1886-1972) was born in Uppkot, Norðurárdalur. She graduated as a midwife in Copenhagen in 1908 and worked in Ísafjarðarkaupstaður from 1909 until 1917, when she emigrated to America (Massachusetts). In 1950, she graduated as a nurse, and worked at a hospital in Boston until 1966. She had already written short stories for *Eimreiðin* and *Iðunn* before she left Iceland. Her later stories have appeared mainly in *Tímarit Þjóðræknisfélags Íslendinga*. A collection of her short stories was published under the title *Margs verða hjúin vís* (Reykjavík, 1956).

"Stones for Bread" is translated from "Steina fyrir brauð" in *Tímarit Þjóðræknisfélags Íslendinga* 5 (1923), pp. 71-78.

EVERY DAY, for ten years – including Sundays – Mrs. Maria Hansen, the wife of Geir, the manager, partner, and chief baker of L.P. Hansen Bakery, had climbed half way up the stairs and called, "Sveina! Sveina, you mustn't fall asleep again." Sveina had answered equally often, "I'll be down in ten minutes," even though she had not begun to dress. As she had uttered the last word, the clock struck half past eight. Her mum never failed to allow her half an hour to dress and to have a little coffee before she went to work at the bakery.

Stína, the maid, brought her coffee at eight, but it was so pleasant to lie back again and doze a little longer, to close her eyes and think about Gunnar; see Gunnar lead her by the hand beneath the mountain, see him dance with her at the Good Templars' Club, and kiss her. Gunnar!

There was no reason to hurry. Her dad worked the first hour the bakery was open, and there was hardly anything to do until after ten o'clock, at least not this time of the year. It was delightful to think about Gunnar in peace and quiet.

She could hardly believe that almost a year had passed since what was most often on her mind had happened.

It was nearly a year since Gunnar had kissed her – since she had sat on his knee inside the cubbyhole at the back of the bakery, the small room which her dad called a retreat and her mum called the office. It was nearly a year since he had invited her to go with him to the Christmas dance. Now it was rumoured that he had invited Dúlla from the pharmacy to this year's Christmas dance.

It was just after Christmas, about three weeks before her birthday – her birthday was on the nineteenth of January, but she would never celebrate it again – that Gunnar spoke about getting married in May. "Then we should become engaged on my birthday," she had suggested; but he was of a different opinion. When his sister's engagement had broken off after two years, he had vowed that the same would not happen to him. They had an argument; finally Gunnar took his hat and left as silent as the grave without saying goodbye. And now someone had seen him out on Króksoddur with Dúlla from the pharmacy!

She and Dúlla had been confirmed at the same time, but Dúlla had moved with her parents to Brimtangi the year after, and then come back when her father received the position of bookkeeper with the consul. And now she washed bottles at the pharmacy and sold castor oil and talcum powder. Dúlla, who claimed Barabbas had been the king of the Jews, and mixed up the Ten Commandments, when she studied for confirmation with the pastor. Now Gunsa from Gísli's store thought that she had seen Gunnar put his arms around her out on Merkisteinn! Was it possible?

Of course, she had pretended that nothing had happened this year. She had to. Their engagement had only been between the two of them, so she had no claim to anyone's sympathy. She wanted to hide, to pretend that nothing had happened. Had she not danced almost every other dance with Lárus, the dean's son, at the dance held by the women's organization Vonarljósið on the Twelfth Night of Christmas and pretended that she was having a really good time?

Not that those who lived in Sandfjörður thought much of Gunnar.

He worked in a store for his father, Mangi the Failure, who had not gone bankrupt but was always on the borderline. Why was she not able to free her thoughts of him? Why was her mind bent upon his every word and action, every smile – each kiss?

Why hadn't she been more compromising about the engagement? She had never noticed it until this year how often her mum said, "Yes, you're probably quite right" – when her dad was firm about something she knew her mum didn't agree with. Too late!

There were no other boys in Sandfjörður – that counted. Lárus, the dean's son, danced admirably and seemed to enjoy dancing with her. Björn, the helmsman on Sigurfari, invited her down into the basement for coffee right after the first dance and didn't seem to be in a hurry. He had even offered her his horse any time she wanted it. Then there was Arnfinnur Jóhannsson! Addi Jóhannsson, the son of the goldsmith. Addi was surely smitten with her, but the funny thing was that she had never done anything to attract him. She had never been other than straightforward and "friendly" with him, just as she was with anyone else who came to the bakery to buy cookies and Danish pastry, even though he had been dropping by lately on possible and impossible errands, and even though he said he was going to the Christmas dance if a certain girl would go with him. Addi, who didn't know any dance but the polka, and not all that well either!

Addi was a steady boy. His parents were thought to be prosperous. Why couldn't she forget Gunnar? What foolishness had come over her? Each time she saw his hands she wanted to touch them. Gunnar!

Was it possible, was the clock chiming nine times? She hurried to fasten the last pin to her bonnet and rushed downstairs.

Her brother Eyjólfur was sitting at the kitchen table finishing his second cup of coffee. "You're not in a hurry to take over for Dad, Sveinlaug, though you know he's been up since six o'clock."

"And neither are you in any hurry to get to the post office, though you should have been there at half past eight."

"Don't start bickering," their mother said calmly. "Don't you want any coffee, Sveina?"

"No, thanks! I've a toothache." She hurried towards the bakery right across the street. She had to refrain from crying. Funny how sensitive she was these days.

"There's been nothing to do all morning," her father said. "I sold for one kroner and ninety-five öre and finished *Martin Eden* – an excellent story." He stretched and yawned. "Try to sell those Napoleon cookies, so that they won't go to waste. – Do you think Mum has kept the coffee hot?" he said on his way out, but didn't wait for an answer.

She folded her shawl and laid it over the back of the chair in the cubbyhole. The cubbyhole wasn't big, but it was the prettiest room she knew, or at least the room she cared the most about. The furniture was sparse and in rather poor condition, but no other would do – for her. There was an old desk, scratched and burned with a framed map of Sandfjörður over it, a chair that swivelled, where Gunnar had sat so often, and a sofa from the factor's estate, full of lumps. She stroked the back of the sofa where she had so often found Gunnar's hand. No, it couldn't be true what she heard yesterday, that Gunnar was engaged to Dúlla. Dúlla – the bell chimed as somebody entered the bakery. "Half a loaf of dark rye bread, a whole loaf of light rye bread, two Danish pastries, six one-öre-cookies." "A whole loaf of dark rye bread, half a loaf of light rye bread, ten one-öre-cookies." People called this life! She walked into the cubbyhole, sat down on the sofa, and closed her eyes. It was quite unthinkable! Had Gunnar not been as completely taken by her as she had been by him? She had been so sure of it. How thick and yet so soft his hair! Brown with a golden shine to it. His lips – oh, so delightful to kiss him, nothing more delightful. How could he be thinking about marrying Dúlla? Marrying!

She had no belief in the power of prayer, and hadn't had for a long time. Perhaps she never had. But all of sudden she knelt down by the sofa, closed her eyes and prayed, "Dear God, if You are all good and almighty, if You are all charity and life, turn Gunnar's mind and heart back to me. Let him love me as before. I don't care about anything else. I shall never ask for anything else. Dear God, hear my prayer! Amen."

She stood up and felt better. She gave Birta from Sölvakot a Danish pastry and three Napoleon cookies when she came back into the bakery, so Birta called her Love and wished her all blessings. It was rumoured that it was beneficial to do Birta a good deed; she was wiser than a witch.

This had to be just a guess of Magnea's, the wife of Helgi the Shopkeeper. She was such a gossip; sometimes there was no basis for what she said. Who knows, he might even phone! There was the phone, close by the door to the cubbyhole. Who knows! She forgot she had expected the same thing at first, day by day, then week by week, and finally month by month. She had waited for Gunnar, and now she had prayed. Wasn't it written, "Ask and thou shalt receive?" – Had she not asked, "Seek and thou shalt find?" – Why not seek? "Knock and the door shall be opened unto thee?" What was wrong with trying?

Gunnar was probably in the store right now. The store was dark and unpleasant. Food, crockery, shoes and all kinds of things were mixed together, though it had gotten a little bit better after Gunnar started there. He had worked in a store for the consulate but left when his sisters married; they had been helping their father, alternately – or so they said. Why not drop in there, when her dad took over for her at three o'clock? Anyhow, she needed some fresh air. So, why not?

Sveina fixed her hair, made a bigger crease in her hat, put on her prettiest apron, the one Gunnar thought the prettiest, put on a cloak instead of the shawl. She was tall and slim and knew that she carried the cloak nicely. She walked up Strandgata, the main street of the town, and turned onto Merkjagata. In the corner house by the sea side was M. Gunnarsson's store; she walked slowly past it. The same picture of Hansel and Gretel, a few cups, saucers, and soothers were in one of the windows, black shoe polish, paper bags of chicory, seamen's mittens and some other rubbish were in the other window, all covered with dust. No, she couldn't go in right away, she'd come by on her way back. She walked past the stacking yard on the other side of the house. The racks, on which the fish were dried, lay in stacks by the fence covered with hoarfrost. She met Nína, the daughter of Bergmann, the treasurer, who told her that Lárus, the dean's son, had just asked her to the Christmas dance. Then she made a detour, so she wouldn't have to walk by the pharmacy, and went out by the sea. She must see Gunnar.

On her way home she went by the store again, looked in, but saw no one. He was probably in the back room; the store was never heated. What should she ask for? Something that wasn't available, but nothing absurd. She must go in. She opened the door; the bell trembled pitifully. There were only three steps to the counter. . . .

Magnús entered the store, stooped, tired-looking and anxious.

"Good afternoon!" she said cheerfully.

"Good afternoon! What can I do for you?"

"You wouldn't happen to have bezique cards?" Had she come thus far in vain? Was Gunnar not in?

"Bezique cards? I don't think we have any. Gunnar! Do we have bezique cards?"

God be praised! He was in!

Gunnar entered the store. She felt the floor move like the consul's pier, when the ships landed. She grabbed onto the edge of the counter. Did he go pale, or was it because he had just shaved? His hair still had the same golden shade. He had been her fiancé. He had kissed her. She smiled half-embarrassed as she extended her hand over the counter to him.

"How do you do, Gunnar!"

"How do you do, Sveina," he said casually and shook her hand. She wanted to hold his hand forever, stroke his hair, stroke the back of his head with her hand, touch the nape of his neck. She felt she could stop loving him, if he had different hair, or eyes, or a different mouth.

"What was it you wanted, Sveina?" Gunnar asked as he pulled his hand away slowly.

"Bezique cards. Lárus, the dean's son, has been teaching me; he learned the game the last time he went south." She fixed her eyes on him. He showed no reaction.

"It can't be played with regular cards?"

"No. It has two of each suit: two queens of hearts, two kings of hearts, two . . ."

"Unfortunately, we don't have any. Have you tried the post office?"

"Not available there."

"A pity. Was there anything else?"

"No. You . . . will come . . . will, of course, be going to the dance on Saturday?"

"Of course! And you too?"

"What else!" She tried to laugh cheerfully. Jón, the town's councillor, entered the store. She turned homewards to sell bread. Bread!

8

She tried to read *Martin Eden* between customers, but half the time she didn't know what she was reading. Why had she gone to see him? What did Dúlla have that made him like her so much? Dúlla was stupid, ignorant, not even pretty. She danced better than Dúlla. She hated Dúlla.

The phone rang, and it startled her. Her voice trembled when she said hello. Addi Jóhannsson answered.

"I've two tickets to the dance on Saturday. Can I offer you one of them?"

"Thank you. But I was thinking of staying home this time around." She didn't know why she said that; she went to every dance, every place where she had a chance of seeing Gunnar.

"They say there'll be an entertaining programme."

"Well, maybe I'll go."

"Will you be in the store tonight?"

"I guess so."

"I was reading *Solomon's Mines,* a really exciting story. Do you want to borrow it?"

"Yes, please."

"I'll drop by tonight."

"Please do."

"Well, goodbye."

"Goodbye, Addi."

Solomon's Mines! Trash that she had read before confirmation! But Gunnar read Bojer and Hamsun, knew by heart verses from *Pan* and *Victoria.* Gunnar!

She lifted the cover of "the servant" in the corner of the cubbyhole, washed her hands, looked in the mirror. Was she really getting so thin? Almost oldish. Would she be only twenty-five on her next birthday? Couldn't it be that she'd be forty-five? Wasn't it twenty years since Gunnar . . . No! This wouldn't do. She had to find something that would strengthen her and increase her appetite.

Addi came just before eight with a big bag of toffees and *Solomon's Mines.* She invited him into the cubbyhole and thanked him heartily for the toffees – toffees that she hadn't even wanted to look at since she was a girl in a short dress. Gunnar never offered her anything but Milka and Sweetmeat.

She was glad the store was busy for the next half hour. Addi could hardly be called entertaining. He never read anything but trash and explained what he read awkwardly. He wasn't unattractive, always well-dressed and clean. His hair was black and thin, almost bald on top, although he was only twenty-seven, one year older than Gunnar. He would probably become bald before he reached thirty-five. He was an only child, and his father was believed to be very prosperous, the main goldsmith and watchmaker in the town. – Mangi the Failure!

Addi had lived in Reykjavík for two years. He started telling her about a film he had seen there. A film full of Indians and revolvers; she couldn't make head nor tail of it. His eyes, which were small, disappeared in wrinkles when he laughed; their colour was like chicory, and she had never liked that colour. Gunnar's eyes were grey. And the Indians galloped skywards . . . He wasn't far from having a double chin. She knew two girls who regarded him favourably – strange taste. His father had given him a house on Skeljagata, a beautiful house. Given it to him for his birthday, when he turned twenty-five. Why had she invited him over – agreed to go with him to the dance? Someone came into the store. It was Begga from the dean's.

"My employer was putting carnations on a couple tonight," she said as she put the change from the five kroners into her pocket.

"Who?" Sveina asked, and slammed the till so it rattled.

"They came alone. I opened the door for them, took her shawl. Absurd habit, not to become engaged like well-behaved people, to marry all of sudden, just as if . . . which was not the case."

A short pause. Sveina caught her breath.

"These days, these young people get married even when they don't have a toilet . . . don't have a patch for their shoes. They intend to stay with Dúlla's parents to begin with, because . . ."

"Dúlla!"

"They can't stay among the multitude of kids at Mangi's, even if they stood on their heads, ha, ha!" Begga looked up into Sveina's deathly pale face. "Once I thought that you and Gunnar would become a couple." Her smile was insinuating.

"Gunnar and me! Ha! Ha! Why not Lalli, the dean's son, Binni, the helmsman, or Nilji Bergmann. I've danced and promenaded with all of them." Faint, she continued, "Addi didn't mind, he knew that I was just leading the gossips astray. Gunnar and me a couple! Ha! Ha!"

"Addi Jóhannsson? Oh! Good night!"

Gunnar married! Married! Dead, lost to her. What was life now? A grey fog, bread dough. It was as if the floorboards gave way beneath her feet; she sank, deeper and deeper. What did it matter! What did anything matter! Get up, sell bread, undress, dress, sell bread – sell stones for bread? And she had prayed to God! GOD!

She went back in to Addi. He continued telling her about the film. She laughed loudly when the main hero threw the Indians, one after the other, over a cliff. What musical laughter she has, Addi thought.

She felt that she could never smile again. Let him talk. What did it matter! Addi was a well-behaved chap, rather boring. But what did it matter? Dúlla would probably have accepted, if he had asked her. Addi had said that she was stupid and rather foolish, some time or another when Dúlla was mentioned. Addi wasn't very clever, but he was held in high esteem as a goldsmith. He was prosperous and didn't drink. What more could she want? Anything was better than people's insinuations about her and Gunnar, which would now fly on the wings of gossip.

She sat down beside Addi on the sofa, picked up his gloves, which lay on the sofa, put them on her knees and stroked them mindlessly, it seemed. Addi laid his hand slowly and hesitantly over hers. She quickly moved her hands away, shrieked, and said that she had burned herself, but in reality it affected her no more when Addi touched her hands than when her dog Snati rubbed himself against them.

"My hands are always cold," she said.

"Warm heart." Addi was serious. "Whoever will gain it will be lucky." He moved closer to her; she didn't move. He gained courage and grasped her hands firmly. This time she didn't pull them away. A few minutes later they were engaged.

Engaged! She was engaged to Addi! The years would pass by slowly, slowly, grey and uninteresting, endless like the last month of winter, calm like the deep pool in the Merki River. She couldn't sell bread all her life, and she couldn't bear to know that Dúlla was bragging. What was Gunnar but an eighty-kroner counter-jumper? Addi was prosperous. She could have bridge parties and chocolate feasts like other gentlewomen in town. She could go to Reykjavík once in a while. Dúlla couldn't afford that. The phone rang.

"You answer it, just for fun," she said smiling.

"Can you hold on a moment?" she heard Addi say.

"It's Kristín, Dúlla's mother. Would you believe that Gunnar and Dúlla got married tonight? He fetched the rings around noon. I thought they were going to become engaged. When she realized who I was, she invited me and the old couple; she's going to invite you too, one o'clock tomorrow, she said."

"Addi! Can I tell her that we are . . . that we have become engaged? So that the town can once and for all hear of an engagement which isn't a public secret."

"Yes, that would be a great idea!" His eyes disappeared in wrinkles. "I must certainly have some rings in stock. Later, I'll make new ones and engrave them. Yes, yes, I'll do that! I'll run and get them, while you speak with her."

"Hello! My hearty congratulations! Yes, thank you, I'll deliver the message. Yes, we'll certainly be there. Should I entrust you with something? You're the first person outside the family to get this news. Addi and I have become engaged. Addi Jóhannsson. Yes, thank you. Yes, there's an epidemic of this, ha, ha! Yes, you can depend on it, we'll be there. Give the young couple my hearty congratulations. Thank you. Goodbye."

She hung up. Someone entered the lean-to in front of the bakery. Addi with the rings! It was true, she was going to become engaged. Her fiancé was coming. Fiancé! – Gunnar!

Translated by Árný Hjaltadóttir

THE SENTENCE

Bergþór E. Johnson

Bergþór E. Johnson (1896-1950) was born in Mikley, Manitoba. He joined the Canadian Air Force in April 1918; otherwise he lived most of his life in Winnipeg as a teacher and a merchant. He was active in the Unitarian Association and in the Icelandic National League. He is the author of a number of poems and short stories.

"The Sentence" is translated from "Dómurinn," which appeared in *Saga* (1926-1927), pp. 31-35. The story was reprinted in Einar H. Kvaran and Guðm. Finnbogason, eds., *Vestan um haf* (Reykjavík, 1930), pp. 529-532.

IT WAS A CLEAR SUMMER MORNING. The sun shone brightly and flooded Lake Ontario with its rays, so that it looked like a sheet of glittering pearls. The distant forest resembled quivering green garlands of flowers swaying in the breeze. The flowers stretched their golden crowns towards the morning sun as if they wanted to say that everything must be beautiful that day. The birds spread their wings in the blue sky as if they intended to fulfill their most buoyant hopes on this mild day.

I was sitting in the opening of my tent viewing all this glory, when the trumpet stirred me from my thoughts, letting me know that now I had better get ready for the morning parade. We all grouped into ranks in front of the tents as usual in the mornings and prepared ourselves for difficult training until noon. But we were more than a little surprised when we were led directly to the main field east of the camp instead of going to the training field north of the tents. There we were detained, but no further orders were given.

The junior officers walked silently and seriously up and down the field, and we sensed that something important was about to happen.

Although we were glad to be freed from training, we were neverthe-less impatient with waiting, because we had the feeling that some-thing was about to happen that we hadn't seen before. Finally, the senior officer of the camps at Long Branch, Captain Earl, arrived. He was arrogant as usual, and as always I felt the self-esteem and the opinion he had of himself for being senior officer of the most splendid camp of the Canadian Air Force shine from him. He gave orders without delay, and we were made to tighten our ranks until we stood close together in rows and formed a big wall around a square area where the officers stood. Now there was silence and peace again. We waited for a while, and even though we were tired of standing motionless, we didn't feel it because of the impatience and the expectation of what would happen.

All of a sudden a certain kind of restlessness came over the group. Those of us who were standing towards the middle or close to the open area of the square could not see what was happening, but we soon found out. In one corner of the square the soldiers stepped aside, and in came a junior officer and three men. The officer brought them to a halt in the middle of the area, and we immediately saw what was going to happen. The man, who stood between the other two, was a prisoner, and the other two were his guards. Sentence was to be passed upon the court-martialed prisoner. It was the first time that many of us had seen or heard a court-martial.

The first thing I did was to look at the prisoner. He was young, about nineteen, medium height and well-shaped. His eyes were big and blue, his forehead high, and his nose straight and rather big. His mouth was fairly small, with thin lips, but the corners of his mouth gave evidence of strength, and his whole bearing suggested that he would show courage if he set his mind on something. His face was now pale and grave, but still he looked undauntedly at the officers and his comrades. The soldier standing next to me was restless, so I looked at him and was about to tell him to stand still; but I was startled – he was white as a sheet and trembled like an aspen leaf. I asked him in a whisper if he was sick, but he said no. I whispered to him again and asked if he knew what this kid was being sentenced for. "Yeah," he answered. "I know. He's my best friend, and two months ago he asked for leave to go home to see his mother, who was on her deathbed. He was refused leave, but he left anyway, and didn't come back until a few days ago. He knew that he'd be court-martialed when he returned, but he claims to be ready to suffer the sentence, no matter what."

We couldn't talk any longer, because Captain Earl started looking through the documents that had been sent to him from the court-martial. No one knew the decision, and I saw the prisoner's mouth pucker slightly when he looked inquiringly at the senior officer. The cap was taken off the prisoner's head and the captain began to read the sentence. We all stood silent and restless, much more restless, it seemed to me, than the prisoner himself. When the preface had ended, the captain stopped for a moment, and then he slowly read these words: "For having been absent without leave from the Royal Canadian Air Force for thirty-six days, the accused, No. 171,638, George Fitzgerald, is sentenced by this court-martial to serve a sentence in the Air Force prison in Toronto, and the sentence shall be 168 days without hard labour. Dated the tenth of July 1918, Toronto."

I kept looking at the prisoner, and when the sentence had been passed he jerked a little and became even paler, but then a sarcastic smile hovered about his lips, and he looked up, and looked at us with blue, sparkling eyes as if he would say, "I'm less ashamed to serve this sentence than I would have been to disobey my deepest feelings and not visit my mother on her deathbed."

The guards led him away, and we went back to the camp. But all nature's beauty seemed to us to have disappeared. It seemed to me as if the flowers bent their heads and shed tears over man's hardheartedness. The birds curved their powerless wings, as if their hopes were still unfulfilled. The waves on the lake seemed to put on a grim look, as if they wanted to snatch all human judges. And the trees seemed to stretch their branches towards the sky as if to ask for more justice on earth. But my thoughts were disrupted when the guards walked past us with the prisoner on the way to the prison. Smilingly, he looked at us and walked with his head held high, as if he felt he had done the right thing and was ready to take responsibility for his actions. We all stopped and cheered him when he walked past to show him that we felt he had won a victory.

Translated by Kirsten Wolf

FELLOW STUDENTS

Friðrik J. Bergmann

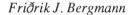

Friðrik Jónsson Bergmann (1858-1918) was born at Garðsvík, Suður-Þingeyjarsýsla, and came to America in 1875. He received his liberal arts education at Luther College, Decorah, Iowa, and his theological training at the University of Christiania (Oslo), Norway, and at the theological college of the General Council of the Lutheran Church in Philadelphia. During the years between 1886 and 1899, while serving as a pastor in Icelandic communities in North Dakota, he was also vice-president of the Icelandic Lutheran Synod and became editor of *Aldamót* (1891-1903). From North Dakota he moved to Winnipeg, where he taught Icelandic at Wesley College and served as a pastor of his congregation, the Tabernacle Church in Winnipeg. In 1906, he founded *Breiðablik* and served as its editor until 1914. Among his main works are *Ísland um aldamótin* (Reykjavík, 1901), *Vafurlogar* (Winnipeg, 1906), and *Trú og þekking* (Reykjavík, 1916).

"Fellow Students" is translated from "Skólabræður" in *Breiðablik* 1 (1906), pp. 29-32. The story was reprinted in Einar H. Kvaran and Guðm. Finnbogason, eds., *Vestan um haf* (Reykjavík, 1930), pp. 254-263.

"HOW ARE YOU, my fellow countryman?" said Sigurður smiling to Skúli as he opened the door to his room, knocking over a chair that stood in the way. Skúli's clothes were hanging over the chair; Skúli himself was in bed. He had just woken up and was reading *The Free Press*.

"How am I? You must have some idea. I've slept and slept and done nothing but sleep since Saturday. I'm still sleepy and could sleep for a whole week."

"That's understandable, you villain. You've stayed awake often enough this last month, both before and during the exams. It's amazing that you've any breath of life left in you. You don't deserve it."

"You've grown a paunch over these last few days, Siggi. Shame on you. You haven't let this affect you. Didn't you care how it went? Do you think you scraped through?"

"I hope so, though I don't know. I'll probably get one or two stars. I don't care. I'll take exams in the fall in the courses I fail now. I'm not going to whine about it. You'll get the prize."

"I don't know. I thought a bit about it during the struggle, especially at night when I wanted to sleep but couldn't. But then I closed my eyes. It's dark in my head, dark around me. I don't care about anything. I hardly know if I'm alive. When I look in a book or a magazine I don't know what I'm reading."

Skúli had started dressing slowly and carefully while he made this confession. He was good-looking – fair, tall and slim, friendly but tired-looking, and his eyes were dark blue and intelligent. He was rather slow in his movements as if his body lacked the vigour and energy that his soul appeared to have.

"Hurry up," said Sigurður as he opened the window. "It's almost noon and you're still lying here. It's better for you to come with me out into the sunshine. The weather is fantastic. Such a day is worth a thousand exam days, even if one got an *A* in every subject." He cast a sidelong glance at Skúli. Vigour and playfulness shone from his eyes. He knew that he had touched a sore spot.

"I'll believe that," said Skúli. "You are and always will be nothing but a sun-devil."

They walked slowly and idly down Portage Avenue. The carriages shot back and forth and the noise resounded in their ears. The sun was so bright that they could hardly look up. They were both in a good mood. Their entire conversation was a cut and thrust of teasing and fun. Both thought that life would win out in the end. Still, Sigurður was much more certain than Skúli. How it would do so was a mystery to both of them, especially Sigurður. He believed it, but knew at the same time that it would take a miracle. He thought it was best to wait calmly until the miracle came and meanwhile enjoy life. Skúli had an unclear suspicion that the exams would be the best way. But he had many, many exams left.

When they came to Main Street, Sigurður stopped in front of a well-known restaurant. "Let's go in and eat, Skúli, like men. The old man gave me a few cents this morning. There's no better way to spend them." They went in and sat down in the innermost corner. Skúli hadn't eaten a proper meal for a long time and had lived like a bum. He owed fifty dollars for food and rent for the winter. Now he no longer ate there. He could keep his room until he left for the summer.

Sigurður suspected all this but didn't want to bring it up. He was the son of a wealthy man who had been in Winnipeg for a long time. The beginning had been hard, but now he owned the moon and stars and wanted to see to it that his children got a good start in life.

"Will you be at home for the summer, Siggi?" asked Skúli as he took a bite of a delicious, spicy steak, full of red juice.

"No," said Sigurður, and became quite sad. "My father wants to send me west to some farmer. He thinks it's healthy. I'll be bored to death for sure. Where are you going?"

"I'm going up to the Lake," said Skúli. "I'm going to teach in a public school over the summer. I'll have to make money somehow; otherwise it'll be a lean winter." They got up from the table, full and content. Skúli was grateful. He hadn't eaten so well in a long time.

For the rest of the day they had fun. In River Park they watched a football game. "Why don't you take up football, Skúli" asked Sigurður. "They make fun of us Icelanders in school because we don't know how to play. And we look like nitwits as a result."

"I don't have the time, and besides I don't really like it," answered Skúli.

In the evening they went home to Sigurður's house. It was in the northern part of the city. Everyone had gone to bed because it was late, except Björg, Sigurður's eldest sister. She was waiting for her brother. She was seventeen years old, went to the Collegiate, and had done much better in her exams than Sigurður.

It had been a long time since Skúli had visited their home. It was magnificent, with downy-soft armchairs that one sank into and almost forgot about everything. Skúli noticed that Björg had grown up. She was quiet and happy and so beautiful that he was lost for words.

The next morning Sigurður went west and Skúli went up to the Lake.

One day during the summer, Skúli's school was closed. A pleasure trip to Strönd had been planned for a large group of Icelanders in Winnipeg. Skúli thought that he could spend the day no better than to go south to Strönd and see if he couldn't find some of his acquaintances from Winnipeg. He was now livelier and quicker in his movements than in the spring. The lake air had strengthened his nerves, because whenever he had the opportunity, he spent his time out on the water. "I think that most of all I want to go out into the water to the fish and be one of them," he had once said to the people with whom he was staying. They found that odd.

When he came to Strönd, or Winnipeg Beach as it is called, there were crowds of people. One train after another arrived from Winnipeg, all packed with people. They streamed out of the coaches like cattle out of a pen and onto pavements and roads with heavy food baskets and all kinds of bags so that one couldn't move.

Skúli didn't know what to do with himself. He wandered about noticing many Winnipeg-Icelanders; but he didn't approach them, because he saw no one with whom he wanted to talk. He deeply regretted having come. It would have been so much nicer to go out on the lake all alone and not be in any crowd.

He sat down on a bench by the beach and looked at the water. It was like a mirror in front of him and the sky was reflected in its bosom. "The water there," Skúli thought, "can truly be called The King's Mirror."

There was a swarm of boats just off the beach. Some of them were big sailboats carrying lots of people that had trouble sailing because there was hardly any breeze. But most of them were small boats, some with two and others with four people, rowing in different directions, slowly and aimlessly, only to enjoy the air and the moment.

There were many Icelanders – young and old, men, women and children. Amidst the English chatter, Skúli heard Icelandic laughter and Icelandic words that gladdened his heart. None of the foreigners was as striking as the Icelanders. They knew how to enjoy themselves when they really got going.

All of a sudden somebody came up behind the bench on which Skúli was sitting and put his hand over his eyes. It was Sigurður and Björg was with him.

"I thought you were out west," said Skúli.

They were overjoyed to see each other. Sigurður had been bored. After six weeks he had packed his trunk and returned to Winnipeg. He had helped in the haying and enjoyed it very much in the beginning. He had gotten blisters on his palms, hard swellings on his arms, and sore muscles all over. But when he was lying on the hayload in the fields on the way home to the farm, he forgot all about sore muscles and sore palms. He found life so enjoyable. And when the load had been brought home he stood up and felt no tiredness. He threw off the hay from the wagon with such energy that the farmer hardly had time to stack it. In between he was not free from being bored.

Then he constantly heard people talk about something that came after haying and which was called *harðvist*. The haying was just a joke in comparison. When that began not much was left of anyone who had got blisters on his hands and strained his arms and back in the haying. At this point it was already getting a bit too much for Sigurður.

The word *harðvist* puzzled him a great deal, but one day he spoke with a girl from Winnipeg who had come to meet her relatives. She spoke to him in English and called it *harvest*. Immediately he understood what *harðvist* meant; it was the cutting of wheat.

About the same time he received a letter from Björg, his sister. She told him about all the amusements in Winnipeg. The show had just ended, and she and the other young people had been there every day. Every one had had a great time and each day had been better than the last. In the evenings they had gone to the amusement park. "Happyland" had been baptized "Munarheimar" in Icelandic. The illuminations were as glorious as in any oriental fairy-tale hall. She had also told him about the planned trip to the lake and that everybody was going.

At that point Sigurður could not resist the temptation any longer and left. His arrival took everyone by surprise, and it cannot be denied that his father was less than pleased. Björg realized she should have written about something else and regretted her letter. But she was glad to have Sigurður back home, because they got along so well.

The two of them were in high spirits. They had amused themselves extraordinarily well. Björg was in a snow-white summer dress with a light parasol in her hand and white canvas shoes on her feet. Sigurður was without a vest, in a thin summer jacket with a broad leather belt around his waist, and a long, golden scarf, which hung below his belt and of which Skúli was half-jealous.

"What's the matter with you, Skúli," Sigurður said, "you're so serious. Haven't you had fun? Why didn't we run into you earlier?"

"I was roaming about here and there on the beach," Skúli answered, "until I got scared of all this crowd and badly wished that I were back home. Since then I've been sitting on this bench dreaming away, sometimes asleep, sometimes awake."

"Let's get a boat and go out on the lake," said Sigurður. "We still have lots of time."

They rowed and Björg steered. Her cheeks were red and she was a bit sunburnt. There was a hint of freckles on her nose. Skúli had never noticed them before. She was in a very good mood, but didn't talk quite as much as usual.

"Aren't you bored up north?" asked Sigurður. "Isn't it boring to be a school teacher? I wouldn't be any good at it."

"It wouldn't be so bad," said Skúli, "if it was possible just to get the youngsters to *understand* and to care about what's being taught. But they haven't been told anything, and sometimes this leads to all sorts of misconceptions."

"What are the people like – the adults?" asked Sigurður.

"Good people," said Skúli, "but they've rarely or never had the chance to get any education; they've only read what they've come across in print in Icelandic, which has either misled them, confused them, or been misunderstood by them, so that their opinions are chaotic."

"I detest all misconceptions and confused opinions," Skúli continued. "It gives me the creeps. Nonetheless I often keep silent, because I know that it's no use contradicting them, but I feel uncomfortable."

"I couldn't care less," said Sigurður, and laughed. "I'd let all of them have their own opinions and beliefs as they please. And the more incorrect and distorted they'd be, the more I'd laugh."

"I can't do that," said Skúli. "It's completely impossible for me. Since I was little I've wanted so badly to understand more. I've never had much fun playing around like other youngsters. To me it seemed better than playing games to try to understand something new every day. I'm convinced that the greatest joy and the most glorious

22

achievement in life is to be able to understand things."

Skúli had spoken with such heated emotion that his cheeks were flushed. Björg had been sitting quietly while Skúli spoke, with her head tilted sidewise, looking directly at him and drinking in his every word with her eyes. It seemed to her that fire was burning in his eyes.

"I think one can understand and have all the joy that comes from understanding," said Sigurður, "and leave others alone. What does it matter to you if they labour under a delusion. It would drive anyone crazy to try to bring each man to his knees and start teaching him to understand."

"I can't bear it when people misunderstand things. In school it breaks my heart when I hear the teacher struggling to make people understand something, and the same fundamental errors and wrong answers are given every day as if it's all been in vain. Isn't it sad?"

"Then your heart has problably been broken a few times on my account," said Sigurður, and laughed.

"I've learned one thing at the school this summer," Skúli continued. "It's just as joyful to make others understand as it is to be able to understand. You should see the brightness in the faces of the youngsters when they come to understand something. Those have been my happiest moments."

Björg looked down at her lap. She looked embarrassed. Had she had enough of this demand for understanding? Or was she trying to hide her feelings?

They had landed and pulled up the boat. As they walked away from the boat Skúli said, "I think I'll go out to some tiny, solitary village, bury myself there, and try to get people to understand."

"You know what?" said Björg. "I've recently been reading Shakespeare, and I've never enjoyed a book so much. There's so much to understand. Often I wrack my brains for a long time, and I'm completely lost. But then a light dawns on me and I understand. It's wonderful."

"Really, Björg? You read Shakespeare?" asked Skúli.

Sigurður looked at him. He saw a gleam in his eyes he had never seen before.

Somebody called to Björg. She gave Skúli her hand and said goodbye.

Skúli's travel companions had gone home because it was late. He had to walk some eighteen miles. But the weather was nice and he said that he liked to walk alone. Sigurður walked with him almost half of the way. Before they parted Sigurður said, "You must not quit school until you've finished. I'll get a loan for you if you need it. Who knows, perhaps you'll make the whole world understand something that has not been understood before, when you've understood enough yourself. And then I'll give you Björg, my sister. You won't find a smarter girl than her. If you two can't make people understand things, I'll be much mistaken."

The sunshine that had been on the lake during the day and that Skúli had called The King's Mirror was in their souls when they parted.

Translated by Kirsten Wolf

"GREATER LOVE
HATH NO MAN THAN THIS . . ."

Grímur Grimsson

Grímur Grímsson (pen name for Björn B. Jónsson; 1870-1938) was born at
Ás in Norður-Þingeyjarsýsla and emigrated with his parents to New Iceland
in 1876. He graduated from the Lutheran Seminary in Chicago in 1893 and
was pastor in Minnesota from 1894 to 1914, when he became pastor of the
First Lutheran Church in Winnipeg. He was a prominent leader in the
Icelandic community and was also active in the larger Winnipeg community,
being twice elected president of the Ministerial Association of Winnipeg,
first in 1925 and again in 1928. In 1921, Luther Seminary of St. Paul,
Minnesota, conferred on him the honorary degree, Doctor of Divinity. Björn
B. Jónsson was editor of *Áramót* 1905-1909, the Sunday school paper
Kennarinn 1897-1901, *Sameiningin* 1914-1932, and of *Vinland* 1902-1903.
    "Greater Love Hath No Man than This . . . " is translated from "Meiri
elsku hefir enginn" in *Vinland* 5:8 (1906), pp. 58-59, 62. The story was
reprinted in Einar H. Kvaran and Guðm. Finnbogason, eds., *Vestan um haf*
(Reykjavík, 1930), pp. 334-345.

It's possible to know of love's power and fame
And charity above all the rest.
It's possible to know how to play the game
Yet lose and still be the best.

The flag over the college building in Middleton was at half-mast,
because the president had died. For fifteen years, Professor Frímann
had been the president of the college and honoured by students and
respected by his colleagues as its heart and soul. He was well-known
and considered among the most learned men in the country.
    Since his youth, Professor Frímann had been an energetic and
hardworking man. As a student, no one surpassed him, except one

whom no one remembered any longer. Ever since he graduated, Professor Frímann had been a teacher. He began as an assistant teacher in mathematics in the college where he had been studying, and a few years later he was made senior teacher in that subject. From then on his reputation grew each day. He was the main force of attraction at the college. He wrote text books that were later used in many other colleges, and his reputation spread over the whole country. When the college in Middleton was established, Professor Frímann was unanimously elected president. He accepted the appointment and left the college in which he himself had studied and taught for eighteen years. The only thing that persuaded him to accept the new position was that he realized that in this way he could accomplish more and thus improve the educational programme of his country. After fifteen years of his leadership, the college in Middleton was now by far the best college in the country, and it was understood that it was primarily owing to Professor Frímann. Now he had died in his early sixties after a long and beautiful day's work. Therefore, the flag was at half-mast and the college in grief.

The funeral was magnificent and lavish as befitted a famous man. All the public places and all the shops in the city were closed on the day of the funeral. The most important men of the country came from all directions to be there. In addition, there were many scholars and academics from far and wide.

The funeral ceremony was held in the biggest church in the city. The church was decorated with flowers and draped in black cloth. Everyone was stylishly dressed and solemn-looking – all except one. There was one man in the crowd who was not dressed for the occasion: an old man, grey and bent, with a beard and long hair, a big man and sturdily built. His forehead was high, and his face was expressive like the waves of colour on a painting. Sometimes an admirable dignity came over the man, sometimes an immense grief, but always an unshakeable steadfastness.

At first, only a few noticed this old man, except that many found it improper that such a poorly dressed man should get to the front pew and be the first to see the corpse when the coffin was opened. Nobody knew him. The only one who might have known him was the deceased, but the dead cannot speak.

He did not bother anybody, the old man in the coarse, western clothes. He sat quietly looking down onto the floor, until the pastor read his text from the pulpit: "Greater love hath no man than this, that a man lay down his life for his friends" (John 15:13). At these words the old man gave a start, and a quiver of pain came over his eyes. But he immediately recovered and sat quietly while the pastor delivered the funeral oration.

The pastor was Benedikt Líndal, the best orator at that time. In beautiful words he described how the primary motive in the life of the distinguished deceased had been his love for people and how he had given his whole life to serve others. He had truly given his life to his friends – the people – and now his memory was so blissful to all those who had known him.

Professor Frímann was buried with great ceremony. A large number of people stood by his grave with tearful hearts. Then everyone went home. But that evening in the dusk, the old, unknown man from the mountains in the west returned to the churchyard and lurked by the grave for a little while. Then he disappeared and was never seen in that area again.

Since then, a magnificent monument has been erected over Professor Frímann's grave, and he has become famous in the history of the country. But no one has heard of the old man who came to his grave, and no one knows where his bones are resting. Still, people might find his story worthwhile.

It was mentioned in passing earlier, that during Professor Frímann's years as a student only one man had surpassed him, a man of whom nothing came and who had been forgotten by everybody. This young man was precisely the strange, old man. His name was Karl Líndal. They had been fellow students and pals for many years, Pétur Frímann and Karl Líndal. They agreed on everything and had grown together in friendship. They were so fond of one another that they could not be apart as is sometimes the case with young men and how it was with David and Jonathan in ancient times. Frímann and Líndal were classmates and ahead of all others in most subjects except mathematics; that was Frímann's best subject. Literature was, on the other hand, Líndal's favourite subject. But Líndal's ability and strength of will was such that he could outdo every man in college in whatever discipline, if he put his mind to it.

Never had such a large and excellent group of students graduated from Concordia University as that spring when Frímann and Líndal graduated. Everyone was certain that Líndal would be number one and receive the highest prize. But when the last months of winter came and those who wanted to compete for prizes and honours at the graduation in the spring should put their names forward, everyone was greatly surprised that neither Líndal nor Frímann registered. Even though the two of them had not discussed the matter, neither one was surprised at the other; both seemed to know that the other did not want to enter, so that they would not be competing against each other. But there was something else that both of them had in mind, although each was unaware of the other's intentions.

In the spring, there would be an opening for an assistant teacher in mathematics at the college. The president had advertised the position around the new year, so that all the younger and older students from the college, that is, all those who had graduated from the college, would have the opportunity to compete for the position. And the one who got the highest grade on the special exam that was to be taken would be chosen. It was no easy task. It seemed almost impossible for any man who had not specialized in mathematics at other colleges since graduating from Concordia. The documents in which the examination was explained were handed out to those who were interested. First, the applicant had to solve in writing many of the most difficult problems in mathematical science, and, second, the applicant had to write an essay that illustrated an original idea in the field of mathematics. It was taken for granted that many of the former students of the college would apply for the position, for it would certainly better the life of the one who got the position and make his future secure, as indeed it turned out. The candidates were to hand in their answers the day after the end of the semester, because on that day the entire college committee would be there. The names of all the applicants would be held confidential and the name of the successful candidate would be the only one made public.

It would take a lot of strength for someone from the class taking finals that spring to also attempt the teacher-exam. Indeed, it generally did not even occur to people that someone might try.

As was mentioned before, Frímann surpassed all others in mathematics, and his self-confidence in this subject was beyond limits.

Therefore, he decided to apply for the position and try the exam but to let nobody know of his intentions.

When Líndal heard about the position and saw it as an open door to a position and to fame for one man, he also decided that he and no other should be the one, no matter what the cost. Admittedly, mathematics was not his best subject, but he knew what he could count on, knew that he could make it his subject, and he had so far never lost in any game he wanted to win. "Five months," he thought, "is a long time, and if I work both day and night, much can be learned in five months."

There were many things that drove him to try to get the position – and the fame. He was poor, and it was clear to him that if he got the position, his financial situation would be improved more than he could imagine. And then there was the president's daughter. It was certainly a step in that direction to stand on an equal footing with her, if he became a teacher. Who knows, perhaps he would one day come so far in life that he could tell her everything he dreamed of, waking and sleeping, tell her about the hope that he now dared not entertain.

He made up his mind as if it were a matter of life or death to apply for the position and to get it.

Never has a man set to work more seriously, and never has a man put his heart and soul into his work more than Líndal. He collected all the best textbooks in mathematics. He calculated all mathematical problems and examined the logic behind them. He only slept an hour here and there. The more time that passed in the preparation, the stronger he felt within himself; and when he started writing the essay he wanted to submit, he felt that he had mastered the discipline. The time passed and the work was completed, and he knew that he would be successful. A new life came into his soul. He felt his boiling-hot blood swell in his veins. In his mind he had become a teacher, and he had come so wonderfully close to his high goal, the beloved image: the president's daughter.

Everyone had been so busy preparing for the finals that nobody paid any attention to the fact that Líndal was rarely seen outside his room. The students had thought about nothing but the exams and had neglected all entertainments and social activity. But then the big day came that no student will forget – graduation day. Then there was merriment. The class that graduated stepped forth to receive their diplomas, and both teachers and students alike thought it strange that he who was undeniably the best of all, Karl Líndal, should not come forward before all those who had received special honours in the exams; but he had not competed for them and looked anything but disappointed. Líndal was in high spirits all day. He knew what honour he would receive the next day. The two friends, Líndal and Frímann, were together for a while later that day. Líndal was so pleased that he did not notice the look of worry on his friend's face. He could hardly keep himself from telling Frímann what was up, but nonetheless he restrained himself and laughed to himself at the thought of how surprised and pleased Frímann would be the next day, when he would hear everything and that Líndal had received the position.

In the evening, Líndal sat alone in his room reading over the essay that had to be turned in to the examiners the next morning. He felt good. He was so certain. His entire soul and his entire life were in these documents. His entire existence was now on paper, and this paper decided whether he would actually continue to exist or not.

There was a knock on the door. Líndal put the paper in a drawer and said, "Come in," and Frímann, his friend, came in.

Frímann sat down, and now Líndal noticed that Frímann looked both tired and nervous. They sat down together by the fireplace and Frímann told Líndal the whole story, that he had prepared to attempt the exam tomorrow and compete for the position.

Fortunately, they had dimmed the light before they sat down by the fireplace; otherwise Frímann would probably have noticed how surprised Líndal was. He blushed, he became hot, he stiffened, but sat still. Frímann took out a big pile of papers, placed them in Líndal's hands and asked him to look at them. He said that he would hardly expect Líndal to understand the essay properly since mathematics was not his speciality.

Líndal took the essay as if in a dream; he mumbled something but hardly knew what he said. Frímann thought that his agitation was because he was overcome with sympathy towards him.

"Don't worry, my friend." said Frímann, as if to cheer up Líndal. "Tomorrow you'll verify that I won't put my friends to shame; return the paper to me tonight with the errand boy when you've finished looking it over." With that he left.

Líndal turned up the light, sat down at the desk, and stared at the paper. At first he could not concentrate on anything that was written, but gradually the words got his attention, and in the end he read with great interest. The soul of the scholar in him awoke, and he read and read and was enchanted by Frímann's excellence and knowledge. It was quite clear that this was a masterpiece. He could not help comparing Frímann's paper with his own. He made himself an objective judge, and the more he compared them, the more he realized how hard it would be to choose between them. Eventually he came to an explanation of a rule about the calculation of the distance of stars in Frímann's paper that was wrong, and then he no longer needed any proof. Frímann was likely to lose and he himself to win. He sprang up from his seat, overjoyed, called for the boy, and sent Frímann his paper.

He knew that he was likely to get the position now that he had defeated even Frímann. There was no end to his joy. He took his paper, wrapped it carefully, and tied a ribbon around it. In this way it would be delivered into the hands of the examiners the next morning, and from these hands he would receive the honour, the position – and finally her. He stroked the paper like a mother strokes the curly hair of her child, and a mother has hardly loved her child more than Líndal loved this offspring of his; it was not only a bone from his bones, but also a soul from his soul.

All of sudden it was as if a sword pierced his soul at the thought of Frímann. Frímann to lose! Frímann his friend, his brother, deprived of his hope. God help him. No, no, Frímann must not lose. In his mind the grief, pain, and anguish that Frímann would feel if he lost, and lost to him, multiplied. Líndal felt he would be a murderer if he took the position, the future, and life from Frímann.

But wouldn't he be committing suicide if he deprived himself of the position, future, life? He was so agitated that everything became much bigger than it really was. He paced about restlessly. The more he thought about the matter, the clearer it became to him that either he had to commit murder or suicide, because he felt that there would not possibly be any life left for the one who lost. Which of them had to lose?

"If the paper on the table is submitted, I'll win," thought Líndal, "and I've seen and read Frímann's paper, and he doesn't even know about me. Would Frímann have competed if he'd known about me? No, he wouldn't. Frímann has priority. He didn't know about me. It's completely up to me to solve this."

No, under such circumstances he could not send off his paper. He could not attack Frímann his friend in this way. Wouldn't that be disgraceful, treacherous murder? Wouldn't that be to steal upon him and stab him in the back? No, never, never would he forsake his friend, never, never betray him.

But wasn't he a coward and a milksop? Isn't this just life? All is fair in love and war. Why should he give way to another man on the chessboard of life? Hadn't he won the game honestly? Yes, indeed. "Frímann takes care of himself, and I take care of myself."

How awfully painful this was!

It was past bedtime. He made ready to go to bed. The Bible lay on the desk. He had never gone to bed without first reading a chapter from the Bible. He had become used to it at home with his mother, and he had retained the habit. Often he had read just because it was a rooted habit, but sometimes what he read had seized him and he had prayed to God like a child. Out of habit, a habit that had become as natural to him as to undress, he opened the Bible. The evening before he had been reading Jesus's parting speech and had made a pencil stroke where he stopped, also out of habit. Now his eyes, again out of habit, searched for the pencil stroke, and the stroke was at the thirteenth verse in chapter fifteen of the Gospel of St. John. And he read: "Greater love hath no man than this, that a man lay down his life for his friends." He read no more. He jumped up and fell to his knees. "Oh, my God, so it is You; You command me to do this!" For how long he knelt by the bed he did not know. Finally, he lay down on the bed, but he did not sleep. Sometimes sleep almost overcame him, but the fire in his heart drove sleep away from him. All kinds of images drifted before his eyes: Frímann as a college teacher, Frímann hopeless and defeated, he himself elected for the position, and her. She was an ambiguous image, hardly visible, and yet so clear. What should he do?

In the early morning he slumbered. He woke up, startled, by hearing what seemed to him someone saying, "Greater love hath no man than this." He got out of bed. The red of dawn was visible on the eastern horizon, and there were still red-hot embers in the fireplace. On the table lay his essay. "Greater love hath no man than this. Greater love hath no man than this."

He took the essay, went to the fireplace, sighed, and let it fall onto the embers. A fire flared up. He looked on. It didn't take long. The fire went out, but the ashes remained. As he stood there staring at the ashes of his hopes, all the wells of his soul dried up, and all the springs of his life clogged.

When he finally turned away from the fireplace, he was a different man – a man who had lost the ability to feel.

He went back to bed and slept very deeply late into the day. When he had dressed and gone to the college, he noticed that everyone was in the assembly room, because there the leaders of the college were going over the applications and exam papers, and everyone was eager to hear how it would go.

Líndal felt no desire to go there. He went up to his room and packed his belongings. He wrote Frímann his friend a few lines saying that he had to hurry home to his mother and could not wait for him. Then he congratulated him on his new position, which he was certain he would get – as indeed he did. Líndal left the college before the convocation was over. He went home to his mother but not to stay. He was no longer content in his old home. After a few days, he went far west, travelling over mountains and through valleys in unknown country. He settled down in a small valley between the mountains. He cleared forest there and mined for ore. His hands became hard and dark, and he became round-shouldered. He never came back east for thirty-three years. Frímann kept inquiring about his friend and longed to see him. He could not understand his hasty departure; but he was never able to find his whereabouts.

Gradually, Líndal came to see newspapers and often he read in his exile about Frímann's glory and prosperity. One day he got a paper in which was printed a telegram announcing the death of the famous professor. Then his soul stirred and he felt again. He travelled all the way to Middleton to be present at the funeral, to see him dead for whom he had sacrificed his life.

This was why the strange old man was present at the funeral of the great man. When Líndal saw the dead body of his friend, the wells of his soul were again filled and the clogged springs freed. This was why he gave a start when the pastor read the text from the pulpit. And this was why he still lurked at the gate in the dusk and shed his first tear of happiness.

Then he disappeared again. Disappeared into oblivion.

It's possible to know of love's power and fame
And charity above all the rest.
It's possible to know how to play the game
Yet lose and still be the best.

Translated by Kirsten Wolf

AT LOW TIDE

Guðrún H. Finnsdóttir

Guðrún Helga Finnsdóttir (1884-1946) was born in Geirólfsstaðir, Suður-Múlasýsla. She emigrated to America in 1904 settling in Winnipeg, where she lived the rest of her life.

Most of Guðrún H. Finnsdóttir's published stories appeared in *Tímarit Þjóðræknisfélags Íslendinga* and in *Heimskringla*. Many of these were later reprinted in *Hillingalönd* (Reykjavík, 1938), *Dagshríðar spor* (Akureyri, 1946), and *Ferðalok: Fyrirlestrar, ræður, æviminningar, erfiljóð*, was published after her death by her husband Gísli Jónsson (Winnipeg, 1950). Guðrún H. Finnsdóttir was also the editor of *Brautin* 1944-1946.

"At Low Tide" is translated from "Undir útfall" in *Heimskringla* 22 December 1926, pp. 2-3. The story was reprinted in Einar H. Kvaran and Guðm. Finnbogason, eds., *Vestan um haf* (Reykjavík, 1930), pp. 514-518.

SOONER OR LATER, all people arrive at the point where they need to take stock of their lives, of themselves, and of their life's work. And tonight Ófeigur from Lundur was taking an account of the debit and credit of just over fifty years of his life. He let the horse walk slowly, at a leisurely pace, over the levelled road. He was comfortable in the soft seat. The weather was mild, there was almost no frost, it was dead calm, and there was a white moon. Everything was covered in new-fallen snow, as far as the eye could see, except where the thicket stood, dark and silent, keeping guard like a regiment of dark elves.

Ófeigur was tall and broad-shouldered, a handsome man, with dark hair, keen eyes, and sharp features. In his youth, he had been a happy man, good-looking and manly; and many a girl in the district had felt her heart beat faster in his presence. Thus it was with all things for Ófeigur. People said it was as if luck followed him. He grew wealthier and more respected with each passing year. But Ófeigur's prosperity was not due just to luck. He had worked like a beaver and never taken a rest, until recently, when he was forced to because of poor health.

He was on his way home from the doctor that evening. They were old friends, and he had told Ófeigur the truth, that his life would soon come to an end. And Ófeigur was not dwelling on it, because it was not his temperament to do so, but his mind was unusually busy tonight. It was not until now, when time had become so precious, that he realized how little he had achieved, how empty his life had been of all things except toil and anxiety over the farm.

It wasn't that he hadn't made money, or gained power and respect in his district, but that as his outer self had expanded and increased, his inner and better self – his emotions and soul – had dwindled and shrunk. Yes, he needed to clear up accounts here and there, but most of all with Sólveig, his wife, whom he had neglected in all his bookkeeping, his wife, who had loved him, looked after him, given birth to his beautiful and promising children, struggled and worked with him all these years.

He was not able to remember exactly when and why they had started to move apart from each other, little by little, ever so slowly. They were both equally concerned about the farm – in that they were united – but married life and the joy in their souls had slowly subsided and had become brooding indifference; finally it had risen like a wall between them, which neither tried to break. Until now, he had blamed this on their temperaments: he was domineering, with a violent temper, and driven by work, and she was stubborn, willful and silent.

But wasn't the same basic cause too much toil, tiredness and monotony, which slowly and surely paralyzed all joy and compassion? And Sólveig had once been cheerful, affectionate and beautiful; she was still beautiful, but her cheerfulness had disappeared. And wasn't he the reason for that? Quiet, serious, in control, and always working, that was her now. Even his mother would have thought it too much, if she had been alive. She, who had been afraid that Sólveig was frivolous and good for nothing, when he became engaged to her. Yes, he had become engaged to Sólveig in defiance of everything and everyone. How he had loved her then, and intended to wait on her hand and foot to the end! But had he always done so?

And now, as he drove leisurely homewards, he could see vividly in his mind's eye that evening when they had become engaged. He could recall every minute detail of that drive. It was ever so different from this one, except that it was on Christmas Eve, just like now. Then his companions were youth, love and future hopes, Sólveig; but now his companion was death.

Arrangements had been made for a Christmas celebration in the small country school, and back then it was the greatest festivity going. His younger sisters and brothers could hardly contain their excitement, and his anticipation of the trip wasn't any less than theirs, but mostly because Sólveig would be coming along. She was his mother's maid and had come from Iceland the previous spring. She hadn't been there very long before he realized that he was in love, and so deeply that he saw his future wife in this poor, orphan girl – if she would accept him. Even then she had a way about her and was able to keep people at a distance when she felt like it. Everything was in a turmoil getting ready for the trip. He had arranged it so that all his sisters and brothers had gone in the big sled; but ahead of the small sled, which held only two, he had hooked up his favourite horse for Sólveig and himself.

It was Manitoba Christmas weather; a clear, starspangled sky, bright moonlight and a motionless calm. The evening was so still and silent; it was as if the night held its breath. There was severe frost, and silvery-white, hard-frozen snow covered everything and rose in waves and crests like a stiffened ocean. Indeed, like the ocean, the prairie in many ways fills the souls of men with a burning desire to wander off to explore endless dimensions. In summer it brings on melancholy, but in winter fear and despair, for when the prairie is covered with snow, it is even more terrible than the ocean, because its tranquility and desolation is even greater. One feels as if death is on the look-out behind every mound of snow. But this time the snow-covered prairie was only a magic place they flew over. The soft snow whirled beneath the horse's hooves, and crunched under the runners on the sled. The air, crisp and cold, burned and stung their faces, and with each breath the frost grabbed their nostrils with its hairy paws.

And out there in the clean, clear and star-filled Christmas night he expressed to her his love and devotion and received the answer his heart desired. And on they flew over the soft, snow-covered prairie – forward as in a dream, alone, all alone in a world of glory, filled with the joy of Christmas and youthful love, with song and joy in their souls. The snow before them was no longer hard-frozen snow, but rather a magic land, upon which good fairies had strewn millions of diamonds that sparkled and shone beneath the evening sky.

The school house was small with a low ceiling, but the tree was big and beautiful, and its fragrance filled the whole house. The decorations were sparse – a few candles and home-made baskets and sweet-filled bags made of diversely coloured paper hung on its branches. The children sang, played and read aloud, and then the Christmas gifts were handed out. And he still remembered the astonishment and joy that shone in her face, when she received the gift he had secretly put on the Christmas tree when he arrived. He also remembered how she had blushed when she opened the parcel and found in it silk for a dress and a little gold pin – from him.

And everyone's face shone with happiness and goodwill, when the people finally prepared to go home. Good night and a Merry Christmas. "Merry Christmas," the people called to one another, when they were outside and the sleds started to slide away. "Merry Christmas! Merry Christmas!" the sled bells resounded, until their echo died out in the distance.

He was home. The whole house was beaming with lights. When he opened the door and walked in, the fragrance of Christmas food met him and blended with the fragrance from a big spruce tree in the living room, which his daughter had just finished decorating. The Christmas tree smiled at him, splendid and glittering with Christmas gifts made of light. His daughter, beautiful, elegant and dressed in her finery, greeted him as he arrived and helped him take off his fur coat. He caught a glimpse of Sólveig in the kitchen, where she was preparing the Christmas dinner. The whole house was polished and decorated – nothing had been forgotten. A festive hue lay over everything; Christmas had arrived.

Christmas guests, friends and relatives from the neighbourhood, gathered there. They were greeted with joy and hospitality and were generously and expertly served. Still, no one was as merry and talkative as the master of the house; he was the life and soul of the party and saw to it that everyone had a good time and that no one was left out. And thus the evening passed in affluence, joy and song, until the last guests said goodbye and the household retired.

The couple were now alone downstairs. Sólveig was moving to and fro about the house, tidying up and adjusting things here and there. But Ófeigur wandered into the sitting-room, where the fire still burned in the fireplace. He sat down in the easy chair by the fireplace, stretched out his feet, and let the warmth encircle him. He was weary after the evening's merrymaking and the burdens of the day. He gazed into the fire and saw the big wooden blocks become red-hot fire and then an extinguished ash-heap. And it dawned on him that there in the fire the trees were returning the sunshine of an entire lifetime, which they had borrowed for their livelihood. Would he live long enough to do the same?

Translated by Árný Hjaltadóttir

HOW I DEFEATED THE LOCAL BOARD

Gunnsteinn Eyjólfsson

Gunnsteinn Eyjólfsson (1866-1910) was born at Unaós in Útmannasveit, Norður-Múlasýsla. He emigrated to New Iceland with his parents in 1876 and lived as a farmer and merchant at Íslendingafljót (now Riverton). He composed music (a collection of his compositions, *Sönghljóð eftir Gunnstein Eyjólfsson*, was published in Winnipeg in 1936), and he is the author of several literary works. These include *Elenóra: Saga frá Winnipeg* (Reykjavík, 1894), *Tíund: Saga frá Nýja-Íslandi* (Winnipeg, 1905), and *Jón á Strympu og fleiri sögur* (Winnipeg, 1952), which is a collection of short stories that originally appeared in various papers and journals.

"How I Defeated the Local Board" is translated from "Hvernig ég yfirbugaði sveitarráðið," which was originally published in *Svava* 2 (1897-1898), pp. 160-171; it is the first of three sketches of the life of Jón of Strympa. The story was reprinted in Einar H. Kvaran and Guðm. Finnbogason, eds., *Vestan um haf* (Reykjavík, 1930), pp. 325-333.

HONOURABLE LADIES AND GENTLEMEN! I intend to begin this story by introducing myself. My name is Jón Jónsson. I'm a farmer here in New Iceland on a farm called Strympa. If I live till the Wednesday of the eighteenth week of summer, I'll be fifty-five years old. In Icelandic sheepskin shoes, I'm five feet and seven inches tall. I won't relate my abilities and physical strength since I myself am the narrator; I'll only mention that I was considered one of the most hard-working men when I was in the prime of life. I've always been in good health – thank God – except that over the last few years I've suffered from rheumatism. It's in the left hipbone and goes right up into the shoulder and won't go away even though I smear myself with arnica and skunk oil.

I hardly expect you to have heard of me, and therefore I've been rather talkative about myself. Here in New Iceland there's a hell of a lot of people by the name of Jón, so that even if I – or one of them – achieve fame, then that fame will never be associated with me or him, because no one knows which Jón it is who did the famous deed. I'll only mention that I'm called Jón of Strympa to distinguish me from other men of the same name – old Jón of Strympa the guys say when they speak of me. In fact, it would be wrong of me to say that I'm totally unknown in the civilized world, because once my name appeared in print. It was in *Þjóðólfur* in 1872 in a notice regarding a red-dappled stallion, the best, which I'd lost and was looking for, that my name and brand appeared. The foal wasn't branded actually, but still I felt it would appear more authoritative to advertise it as such: "Jón Jónsson, Little Strympa, 20 November, branded Jón J." I cut out the notice with my name and have used it as a bookmark in the Gospel according to St. John; it's at the sermon for the sixteenth Sunday after Pentecost (about the dropsical man).[1]

Oh yes, I'm forgetting something. I subscribe to *Lögberg*, and on it my name is printed on a dark-purple label on the cover of the paper every week. I like the labels and have taken them off and kept them, and Ásdís – that's my wife – has glued them with paste onto all my books. The rest I save in my old tobacco cans, because I've completely stopped using them since Grímur Einarsson gave me the snuff horn.

I mentioned earlier that my wife's name is Ásdís. She's three years older than I am and a very talented and respectable woman. She's the stepdaughter of Þorsteinn, who lived at Yxnaþúfa for a long time – a man of honour and a good farmer. I'm surprised that *Sunnanfari* never had a picture of him because he had a superior cow that gave milk every year.[2] My Ásdís was the eldest of the sisters. She was of Danish descent, the offspring of an outstanding bull, and all the farmers in the district competed for the heifers she dropped. I never knew how it came about that Ásdís and I went to America. The district administrative officer, an honourable and fine man, lent us exactly three hundred kroners when we left and never demanded the money back.

Ásdís and I have always gotten along well, but, of course, I'm easy to get along with. If we've been about to have an argument, then I've always given in, because it's not my nature to contradict her. I don't recall her being angry with me except once. It's many years ago. I'd just finished sowing corn in a spot east of the cowshed – at that time I hadn't learned the proper farming methods here – and because the birds were after the corn I set up a big cross-mill[3] to chase them away. But what happened? When I got home, Ásdís bawled me out with such a shower of accusations that I couldn't get a word in. She said that I'd set up the cross-mill in order to dishonour her, because Anna of Snydda had said that Ásdís of Strympa jabbered away day and night like a cross-mill – exactly like a cross-mill – and if I didn't take it down immediately, I wouldn't taste food for a whole week. That I couldn't endure, because food means everything to me. (We eat less these days, and mostly just live on coffee.) I took down the cross-mill and destroyed it.

Ásdís and I have now lived in New Iceland for twenty years. During the first years it was very good to be here, because then there were no taxes and no local board, and I'd managed to get four cows and a few sheep. I owned various other things and a decent bull that was used by the other farmers around. I bought his mother from Jón in Fagrihvammur – a beautiful creature that thrived with us, because Ásdís takes better care of cows than any other woman around. The only problem with the cow is that it has only three teats. I didn't know anything about the local board until the summer when I was told that we had to pay tax, as at home, for the poor, the priest and the administrator. My first thought was to try and see if it wasn't possible to get relief, as at home, but I was told that it was out of the question and that if we didn't pay the tax, we'd be in trouble. So, in the autumn the gentlemen sent us the tax bill, and I can't deny that I got scared. I had a claim to some money for the loan on my bull and got it and paid the tax. Ásdís and I dared not do otherwise, because we didn't know how to deal with the local board. Next year the tax was higher, but I paid it nonetheless by selling my sheep, the one with the black face and the dusky belly, and then I slaughtered a few hens and sold them to the brothers and got a few cents for them.

I didn't know why, but during these two years the number of animals dropped considerably. Hálfa was without a calf, so we slaughtered her. One of the damned things that the local board did to us was to introduce a law that bulls were not to go loose, so I had to kill my bull; by then he had become handsome and fat, but I didn't have any hay to give him. Then thistle started growing in the garden, and we completely stopped seeding it, because Grímur had told Ásdís that nothing could grow in thistle-infested soil, and that it was best to fence it in so that it could grow in peace, and so I did. My old nets became useless, and I couldn't get new ones.

The third year the tax was higher than before and our finances were worse, and one day when Ásdís and I were drinking coffee, she said to me, "With what are you going to pay the tax this year, Jón?"

"I . . . I don't know," I said. "I'll slaughter the ram and use it towards the tax."

"And be without a ram. You probably think that the sheep get lambs by themselves. That's typical of your farming abilities. I think the best thing to do is not to pay tax like Grímur did last year, and he doesn't seem to have been hanged yet."

"Perhaps they'll take the cow away and sell it for the tax."

"You're a fool, Jón, and you always have been since I married you. I'm not afraid of these gentlemen, even though they have their noses in the air. Grímur came today for advice about his cow that had lost the calf six weeks before its time, and says that the local board has given him permission to work off the tax, because he can't pay it in one sum. And perhaps it wouldn't be a bad idea to dig a furrow extending from the deep well and work off the tax in this way. You might get a bit of hay out of it."

"Maybe they'll allow me that if I ask."

"Not if you're stupid enough to pay. If you don't pay anything then you'll get permission, because what can they take away from us? I think it would be easier for us to have fewer cattle; we'll manage in one way or another, and nothing can be taken away if we own nothing."

I realized that this was true. It didn't occur to me to contradict Ásdís. I didn't pay any tax that fall, and nobody said a word. Next year I was charged double tax with interest, and it was impossible for me to pay, even if I'd wanted to. I kind of wanted to dig a furrow from the deep well out to the lake, so I went and asked the local board for permission to work off the tax and told them how difficult Ásdís's and my situation had become.

They gave me permission immediately, because they realized I couldn't pay. I dug a twenty-fathom-long furrow, two-feet wide and one-foot deep, and worked on it for eight days. I found that kind of work hard, although I didn't work very hard at it, and I decided never to let myself be treated like that again by the local board.

The next two years I didn't pay anything. In the first place I couldn't, and in the second place I saw no reason to pay. No one mentioned it, and Ásdís said that it was blasphemous to pay such an ungodly amount to those devils.

So three years of tax piled up. I think it must have amounted to more than twenty dollars. I'd completely stopped complaining about the debt and didn't care, even though the tax bills were coming. Then, one day, when Ásdís and I had just returned from laying nets it happened that Grímur Einarsson arrived, and while he was waiting for the lukewarm, weak coffee, he said to me something like, "Listen, chum, have you heard that the local board has elected a collector to go around and seize our goods in payment for the taxes?"

I was taking snuff and was so startled that I dropped the tobacco I had on the back of my hand. Ásdís was ready with an answer before me – she's hardly ever at a loss for an answer.

"Now they're showing their true colours. Are they now going to sell everything we have, or what? They must be hard pressed if they plan to go into the cowshed at Strympa while old Ásdís is still in good health and standing on four feet. It's all your fault, Jón. You could have slaughtered Rindla, so that they couldn't take her. And if one has nothing, there's nothing to take. Do you owe them any tax, Grímur?"

"Well," said Grímur, "I don't think so. The year before last I worked it off, and last year they let me off. I'll probably owe them the tax for this year, but – I'll never pay it." He said this conceitedly, and I'm sure he meant it. Grímur is no fool, and they will never gnaw at a fat bone from him.

Some days later it happened that as I was mending the goldeye net tatters, I looked out of the window. And I saw him coming, the sinful publican, as the evangelist Sirach calls him, and immediately I knew his errand. I looked at Ásdís and said something to this effect:

"Ásdís," I said to her, "now you have to answer, but try and make sure that he doesn't take Rindla or the ewe; it would be better to slaughter them and eat them."

"You ought to have had the courage to do that already," said Ásdís, and then she stood in the doorway when the sinner arrived. My, my!

I knew a long time ago that my Ásdís had the gift of the gab, but I'd never imagined such a flow of words. The words – and what words – came out of her with such a speed that the tax collector couldn't get a single word in edgeways. And her arms went like – like – well, like a cross-mill, and there is no need to go into detail about how he slinked off and never returned. I smiled to myself over his visit. These gentlemen won't get away with bawling out my Ásdís, even though they may think they can.

We slaughtered Rindla in the autumn and put the money for Rindla on our account for Christmas purchases. We had one heifer that was to give birth in February, and I saw she had stomach trouble and couldn't live. I saw no reason to wear myself out by having two cows; it was difficult enough as it was.

I've received a tax bill every year, but I've disregarded them. My debt is now more than forty dollars. The other day I got damned scared, because I heard that they intended to cut down all the debtors in the district at a meeting, so I went to see Þórður in Framnes – from Keita in Skagafjörður – and I said to him, "Don't you think, pal, that you could go north to the meeting and tell me what they're going to do about me."

"All right," said Þórður and dried his nose with his sleeve. "I'll certainly do that for you."

He went. They sat there at a meeting with the collectors and were taking the necessary steps regarding the debtors of the district. When it was my turn he said, "Old Jón of Strympa owes forty-one dollars. What are we going to do about him?"

They looked at one another, and it was as if the head of a sucker had been popped down their throats.

"There's nothing we can do about this Jón of Strympa, except cross him out of the book. It's a disgrace that names of such men appear in it, and his wife's the worst hag in the whole district. We may be thankful if we never hear of them, because they've completely stopped scraping a living."

I was overjoyed when I heard this. To be honest, I'd always been nervous about the tax. But Ásdís said that she couldn't care less; she'd never have paid it anyway.

This is the way to deal with these charlatans on the board. One must get the better of them. Finally, I must note that I didn't scrawl these lines in order to become famous or to get a reputation as an author. But I considered it my Christian duty to inform my fellow brethren what kind of farming is most advantageous here in New Iceland and how to have a good life and get rid of this monster of a local board; and that is to own nothing and do nothing.

So, now I'm rid of the local board. I've a good life and own one goldeye net, which I put in the lake when the weather's good. I've three cattle: Ásdís's contribution to our livelihood (the one from Þórður's black bull), Hringur and Skakkhyrna. There are five sheep, all from the black-faced one from Jón. We have six hens and one cock (with a double comb) in a pen behind the bed. We're content and worry about nothing, because Ásdís says that as long as the grocer gives us credit, we needn't fear anything; but when he stops, then the local board will "hear of us," as they said at the meeting.

In conclusion, I wish to thank you, honourable ladies and gentlemen, for having listened to my story. If you wish to settle down here, you'll never regret it, although you may have to make use of the wisdom this story contains.

Translated by Kirsten Wolf

NOTES

[1] The story of Christ's healing of the dropsical man is in Luke 14:1-11.

[2] "lagði saman nytjar tvisvar á ári" emended to "lagði saman nytjar á hverju ári".

[3] The Icelandic "krossrella" (here translated as "cross-mill") is a scarecrow. It consists of wing-shaped, crossed sticks, which are placed on a tap and turn in a breeze.

AN ICELANDIC GIANT

Jóhann Magnús Bjarnason

Jóhann Magnús Bjarnason (1866-1945) was born at Meðalnes in Norður-Múlasýsla. He emigrated to Canada with his parents in 1875, settling in Halifax County, Nova Scotia, and later in Winnipeg. He was a school teacher in the Icelandic settlements of Manitoba from 1889 to 1922, with the exception of two periods, the first of which he spent as a teacher in North Dakota (1904-1905), the second of which he worked in a business office in Vancouver, British Columbia (1912-1915). From 1922 he lived in retirement in Elfros, Saskatchewan.

Jóhann Magnús Bjarnason wrote the novels *Eiríkur Hansson* (Copenhagen and Akureyri, 1899-1903), *Brazilíufararnir* (Winnipeg, 1905), *Í Rauðárdalnum* (Akureyri, 1942; it originally appeared in the journal *Syrpa* 1913-22), and *Karl litli* (Reykjavík, 1935). In addition, he wrote a fair number of poems and short stories, most of which appear in *Kvæði* (Winnipeg, 1887), *Sögur og kvæði* (Winnipeg, 1892), *Ljóðmæli* (Ísafjörður, 1898),*Vornætur á Elgsheiðum* (Reykjavík, 1910), and *Haustkvöld við hafið* (Reykjavík, 1928).

"An Icelandic Giant" is translated from "Íslenzkt heljarmenni" in *Vornætur á Elgsheiðum*, pp. 132-46. The story was reprinted in Einar H. Kvaran and Guðm. Finnbogason, eds., *Vestan um haf* (Reykjavík, 1930), pp. 291-304.

I WANT TO TELL YOU a little story from Nova Scotia. It is not brilliant, not an "exciting" tale, and it has no masterly descriptions or literary elegance. But it shows that some traces are still to be found of the ancient Icelandic strength, courage and determination that defied everything, even the elements and death itself. For this story is about a small event, or episode, from the life of an Icelander, who in the fullest meaning of the word can truly be called a giant and had the strength of a troll. And he died only a few years ago.

49

His name was Hrómundur, this Icelandic giant, Hrómundur Þórðarson. He was from the East Fjords of Iceland, and emigrated to America in 1875 with a sickly wife and six children, all very young, and settled on the eastern shore of Nova Scotia. He was then in his late forties.

Although I rarely saw him, I remember him better than any other man I got to know in my youth outside my family. And now I shall give a little description of him.

He did not seem very tall when he was standing by himself, but he was nonetheless a good six feet tall. So stocky was he around his shoulders and body that his stoutness made him seem smaller. I saw him among Scotsmen who were taller than him, but no one was as thick-set and strong-looking. I saw him also among Irishmen, who appeared stouter than him, but that was because they were fatter and not as round, and he was always a big-boned man. I have seen bigger shoulders than his, but never a broader back, and no one with thicker arms nor more broad-chested. His neck was enormously thick, and for that reason his shoulders did not seem as broad. All his joints were large, and the muscles on his arms and legs were exceedingly big, compact, and as hard as stone. His hands were not big in the same way, but they were thick and strong and with continuous small scars and cracks, which showed that they had not been idle in his life.

His face was far from handsome. His forehead was low and covered with numerous wrinkles. His eyebrows were hairy, heavy and big, and almost terrifying. His jaws were long and strong. His nose was rather thin and high and not well-shaped. But his eyes showed that he was of Norse descent. They were blue – sky-blue – hard, cold and piercing. It is said that men who have such eyes are usually dutiful sons, good husbands, the best of fathers, friends to their friends, and faithful. On the other hand, they are always unwieldy and moody when something wrong is done to them, and then they do not spare anyone. Hrómundur had fair hair, a little curly at the back. On his cheeks and chin he had a big, fair and almost invisible beard, which was seldom combed or taken care of. And when he was silent, he pressed his lips together; it is said that this is an unfailing sign of discreetness and firmness.

He was not really an intellectual, a man of letters, and therefore not a scholar. But he often showed that he had a good store of the prudence that is worth having, and he was remarkably practical and clever in many ways.

This, then, is a rough sketch of Hrómundur. When I was a boy and read the old Icelandic sagas, I often thought about him. I did not find him similar to Gunnar or Grettir or Skarphéðinn, but I often thought that Egill Skalla-Grímsson was like him, not because of Egill's wisdom and enterprise, but rather because of the vigour, the temper, and the supernatural strength that they had in common. I never saw him dressed in anything but red canvas clothes, patched all over, which did not suit him, because the trousers were too short and the smock too tight, but then he was also far from being what Americans call a dude.

Hrómundur did not settle in the Icelandic colony in Nova Scotia, but took his abode on a small, barren island outside the inlet called Spry Bay. This island is called Sailors' Woe and is scarcely 100 acres in size. On the western side it is low and sandy, but on the eastern shore very high cliffs rise up. The Atlantic Ocean beats these cliffs all year round, and the sea there is hardly ever calm. The surf roars continuously, day and night, and many ships have been wrecked at the foot of these cliffs and on the reefs in front of them. This is why the island is called Sailors' Woe.

This was the abode that Hrómundur chose – solitary, desolate and rugged, like himself.

The island was far too barren for Hrómundur to support himself and his family on farming. One might say that it gave him "stones for bread and serpents for fish." He had one cow and a few sheep. In order to be able to live there, he had to fish, and fish hard. He even fished at the furthest fishing grounds in a big two-man boat, and rowed alone, and rowed hard like Ingjald and Terje Vigen. One might say about him as Ibsen says in his verse about Terje:

There was a strange man, his hair a grey hue
Who lived on an isle in the bay
He was known to be wise, but words he had few,
And he was mostly at sea every day.
But if he knew of a wrong, he knitted his brows,

And all in sight must their fears assuage,
For 'twas said his anger soon turned to blows,
And no one wanted to be among the foes
Of Terje Vigen and his rage.

Hrómundur took his catch to the trading post in Spry Bay and sold it there. There he was considered a man among men, and everybody liked him. Irishmen and Scotsmen lived there and were considered uncommonly strong men and good sailors, but few of them had cared to test old Hrómundur's endurance to the utmost. The younger men found his grips rough when they wrestled with him, although it was just for fun. There the O'Hara brothers lived, the O'Brian cousins, the McIsaacs, and the Reids; and there the troll Donald Gaskell lived, one of the bravest men in eastern Canada at the time. Donald usually did not praise men for valour unless there was a particular reason; but he always said about Hrómundur that he was "a man," and that was a compliment, because Donald did not call everyone "men." Most men, although they were well capable, were in his eyes "boys" or even "wretches."

"He's a man, that old Icelander," said the giant Donald Gaskell; "he's a man, my boys, he is a *man!*"

But now I shall relate the episode that I promised to describe. It was an achievement, or rather foolhardiness, unique in the history of Western Icelanders – a foolhardy undertaking that no one would dare do except he who has genuine Norse blood in his veins and all the characteristics of a Viking combined in the right proportions. I shall now relate the story as I heard it, or as it is told, like a kind of folk tale, out east by the sea.

One day in the autumn of 1882, Hrómundur's wife fell ill. In the morning of that same day, there was a terrible northeasterly storm. Such storms are common in the autumn in Nova Scotia, and cause the wreckage of many a ship on the shores of this country.

As the day passed, the woman became more and more ill, and the weather worsened constantly. The Atlantic Ocean crashed with all its weight on the shore, the sea raged, the foam-crested waves of the shallows rose towards the sky, and the surf seethed and swelled by each promontory and skerry. And so the day turned into evening, and the woman became increasingly worse, and the weather and the sea raged furiously.

It was now clear to old Hrómundur that it was urgent to seek a doctor, and without delay. He knew that in the village of Spry Bay there was a young and clever doctor by the name of Patrick. But it was five miles to Spry Bay, and it was not a pleasant task to go there in such seas and in such a violent storm. It was simply quite impossible to get there that night, but he hoped that the weather would break in the early morning and that then he would be able to set off.

He did not sleep a wink that night, and he waited impatiently for the day; but when it finally dawned, the weather was no milder than the day before. And the woman was now at death's door. Hrómundur knew, or presumed to know, that nothing would save her life except the help of a doctor, provided he came soon. He realized he would have to risk his life to reach land and fetch Dr. Patrick; otherwise the woman would be dead by the evening. At least he thought it probable.

Three times he went down to the sea, and three times he returned to the house. It was terrifying to look out over the sound. He looked at the dying woman; he looked at his six children, young and small; they were pale and thin and stood whimpering in a group near their mother's bed. The outlook was grim. It was doubtful that he would reach land alive. For a while he hesitated about whether to leave or to stay at home. If he did not leave, his children would be without a mother by the evening. But if he set off, he might well lose his life in the sound, and then his children would be completely orphaned and helpless in an empty house on a desert island, and that was even more deplorable. He pondered this for some time without coming to any real conclusion. Finally, his invincible courage and daring got the upper hand. He had to get to land, no matter what. He said goodbye to his wife and children, pulled out the big two-man boat, and rowed out from the little bay in the west and into the furious surf and the rough sea and directed his course straight to the village of Spry Bay. He rowed with the wind at his back rather than against him.

In the village of Spry Bay, people stood by the sea and looked out over the sound. There is a narrow and long headland to the east of the inlet and it forms a safe and good harbour. The sea is always calm there in a northeasterly wind. But beyond the headland the sea is usually rough, even when there is no wind. The notorious Spry Bay current runs there, and anyone who crosses it alone in a boat in a northeasterly storm is not considered a laggard.

There they stood down by the harbour, the people of the village. There they were, the O'Hara brothers, the O'Brians, the McIsaac cousins, the Reids and the troll Donald Gaskell, all giants and skilled sailors. But they did not like the sea that day.

"What's out there on the sound?" someone asked.

"It's a boat," said Donald Gaskell. He stood with his arms folded, smoking a short clay pipe.

"A boat that puts to sea today must be well-manned," said one in the group.

"There's only one in the boat," said Donald Gaskell, "and that's the old Icelander, because the boat is coming from the island."

"He must be mad," said the others.

"No, he isn't mad," said Donald, "but something must be wrong, because no one puts to sea in a small, open boat unless it's absolutely necessary and someone's life is in danger."

The people of the village stared at the boat. They saw that it was being rowed with great skill and that he proceeded well, and indeed the wind was behind him. He came closer and closer until he came to the surf by the headland. The struggle was hardest there, and for a long time it was doubtful if he would make it. But eventually he got through the current and into the calm waters this side of the headland. Men were ready there and waded into the sea and pulled the boat with Hrómundur ashore. People crowded around him and asked what had made him sail out in such a storm.

"Dr. Patrick! Dr. Patrick!" said Hrómundur, and jumped out of the boat. He was in his old, red, canvas clothes and was bare-headed.

"Dr. Patrick lives up there on the slope," one of the men said. "But what do you want with him. Who's ill?"

"Dr. Patrick! Dr. Patrick!" was all Hrómundur said. He gently pushed the men aside and started walking up the slope to the doctor's house, taking long strides.

Dr. Patrick was in his clinic. He saw this terrible, ancient giant come rushing up the steep slope as if it were a completely flat racetrack. He immediately recognized the man and seemed to know what his errand was. Dr. Patrick felt an unpleasant chill all over his body.

Here it must be mentioned that Dr. Patrick was just past thirty, rather small in stature, but well-shaped, with a pale face, and raven-black hair.

When Hrómundur came to the house, he knocked on the door. When it was not immediately opened, he opened the door himself and went uninvited into the room to the doctor; it was a habit of the Vikings in ancient times and was thought to be a sign of boldness. Hrómundur probably also regarded the doctor's office as a public place, not a private house. And in some ways he was quite right.

"How do you do, Doctor," said Hrómundur. "My wife's ill – come with me out to the island immediately, and I'll pay you whatever you ask for your trouble."

"But the weather is wild, and it's impossible to sail on the sound," said Dr. Patrick. "I can't go with you before the weather breaks."

"My wife's very ill," said Hrómundur.

"To sail out on the sound today is as good as committing suicide," said the doctor, "but as soon as the weather improves, I'll go with you."

"My wife's dying," said Hrómundur in his broken English, "and you must come immediately."

"Even if all the riches of the world were offered to me, I wouldn't go out in this weather," said Dr. Patrick. "No, neither for the King nor the Pope would I go to sea today."

"But the woman will die," said Hrómundur, "and there are six children, young and small."

"I also have a wife and children," said Dr. Patrick, "and I can't run from them into certain death for no reason. I tell you once again that I won't put to sea today."

Old Hrómundur said no more. He became pale, pressed his lips together, and glowered; his eyes flashed and became sharp, hard and terrifying. To Dr. Patrick it seemed that his broad chest swelled and a few big tears ran down his wrinkled cheeks. But they were not normal tears, not the disconsolate tears of the defeated man, but the bitter tears of the hero, the Viking – tears that look like hail – hard, cold and piercing like death.

Hrómundur was formidable as he stood in front of Dr. Patrick. His face twitched strangely, and an awful gleam appeared in his sky-blue eyes; he clenched his strong, rough fingers into his palms so that his knuckles became white, and it was as if each muscle and nerve in his arms and shoulders were seized with cramp. He took one step in the direction of the doctor – and then stood still. In his mind two strong forces were struggling for superiority: reason and audacity. He took another step and stood still. The doctor became nervous. And the giant took one more step and stood still. At the same time reason got the upper hand in his mind, and his feelings and emotions regained their equilibrium. His face returned to its normal colour, and the dangerous gleam disappeared from his eyes. He turned around quickly and suddenly, walked briskly out of the house, went down the slope in a few steps, and then strode in the direction of the boat on the shore.

No one must think that he intended to hurt the doctor. He had something else in mind, as you will soon hear.

The people of the village were down by the sea. They stepped aside for Hrómundur as he walked to his boat. They found his expression threatening, and thought there was something troll-like and unrestrained about him. And they seemed to know the reason.

Donald Gaskell took the clay pipe out of his mouth, went over to him, and placed his hand on his shoulder. "Stay here, old Icelander," said Donald in his deep voice. "Stay here with us until the weather breaks a little, and then the ten most able boys here will take you and Dr. Patrick in O'Hara's boat to the island. Right now no ship can sail on the sound except a big steamer."

Everyone supported Donald, and asked Hrómundur to wait until the weather had calmed down a little. Old Hrómundur was silent. He pushed out the boat very slowly, inch by inch, and appeared to be making up his mind about whether to leave or stay.

"Take my advice, old Sea Wolf," said Donald, "and stay here, because hard as it was to reach shore, it'll be twice as hard to return." But Hrómundur was still silent and continued to push out the boat, inch by inch, without any noticeable difficulty. The boat seemed as light as a shell in his hands.

Just then Dr. Patrick joined the group. Again and again he called to Hrómundur asking him to use his senses and not go before the wind had dropped, and said that then he would go with him. A few others put in a word, but Hrómundur remained silent. Now he had almost launched the boat. He very slowly turned around and looked at the people who stood in a close group on the shore. He looked towards the island and thought about his dying wife and his little children, and he looked at the white foam by the headland and the waves on the sound. In short, he looked like a man who intends to jump over a bottomless chasm, risking his life, and is measuring with his eyes how long the jump is, and considering it doubtful that he will make it.

All of sudden he darted forwards, like only those who are half-trolls and have supernatural strength can do. He leapt up the shore, like a panther or a tiger, and moved towards Donald Gaskell. But when least expected he took another direction and turned quickly into the crowd, to where Dr. Patrick stood, and snatched him with a dreadful resolution; he took him in his arms like a little child, jumped with him into the boat, placed him at the stern, pushed from land, took the oars, and rowed like mad.

Hrómundur's action came so suddenly, and took everyone so much by surprise, that no one had really found his bearings before the boat was afloat. None of these immensely strong men had had the opportunity to hinder the giant in the slightest. When the boat had left land, it was as if they all had awakened from a dream, not least when they heard that Dr. Patrick was calling for help. Everyone ran to the boats that were some distance away on the shore, and many of them in boatsheds. But when they came to the first boat and were about to push it out, they saw that Hrómundur was rounding the headland and heading into the open sea.

"It's too late to pursue them now," said Donald Gaskell, and he knew what he was talking about. "They've already got out into the open sea, and that'll be their death and yours too, if you try to get Dr. Patrick out of the old man's hands, because he'll hold on to him as long as possible. The boat will turn over in such a rough sea if you make such an attempt, and it's better, though bad enough, that two men be lost rather than ten or twelve. But the old giant will reach the island, because he knows the sea better than we do. He's a man, my boys, he is a *man*. Let's allow him to have his way from now on."

People realized that it was true what Donald said and that it was completely useless to pursue them in order to get Dr. Patrick out of Hrómundur's hands. Some people wanted to have the biggest boat in close pursuit, but others tried to talk them out of it, because Hrómundur might not be as careful if he saw a boat come after him. People completely gave up the idea of following them. All the binoculars in Spry Bay were thoroughly used that day. And everyone was glad that the doctor's wife and both his children were not in the village while this took place.

When Dr. Patrick was finally able to raise himself up in the boat, he saw that he had come so far from the shore that there was no chance of his wading ashore, even if he threw himself out of the boat, and he could not swim. The first thing that occurred to him was to call for help. He saw the men ashore run to the boats, and for a while he hoped that they would come to his rescue before Hrómundur rounded the headland. But that hope failed. He cowered in the bottom of the boat, expecting to die any minute, and prayed long and fervently.

Suddenly he noticed that there was a lot of water in the boat. He considered it his duty to make a small attempt to rescue his own life by taking the bailer and starting to bail. He saw that they had crossed the current and were on the sound and that the weather had started abating; but the waves were rather big for such a small boat.

Dr. Patrick started bailing and did a good job; and he found that his courage grew. Now and then he looked over to the bench where the giant sat and rowed for their lives. The rowlocks creaked, the boards and the benches creaked and squeaked and cracked, and the oars bent as if they were just about to break. They were genuine Icelandic iron grips that held these oars. And the strokes were vehement, because the man used all his terrible strength and rowed constantly. He pressed his lips together and did not utter a word, but the sweat flowed from his forehead and ran in streams down his face and onto his chest. The boat only moved forward a little with each stroke, but it gradually advanced nonetheless. They came closer and closer to the island. Hrómundur rowed incessantly and Dr. Patrick bailed incessantly. Finally, they were in the shelter of the island and the struggle was over. When they landed, Dr. Patrick noticed that blood had burst out from under each of Hrómundur's fingernails.

When they got to the cottage, it was getting dark, but the woman was still alive. Dr. Patrick now set to work, and the next morning the woman was out of danger. Now Hrómundur had seven children.

When day came, the weather was good, and about nine o'clock Hrómundur's boat landed once more in Spry Bay. People noticed that Dr. Patrick's hair had turned white like an eighty-year-old (or at least so the story goes out there in the east), but old Hrómundur was the same as always – quiet, silent, cold and ancient-looking – and people saw that he was really fond of Dr. Patrick and that Dr. Patrick had forgiven him with all his heart.

It was Donald Gaskell who proposed that the people of the village get together and offer Hrómundur a good log house in the village and buy him a few acres of land, so that a similar event would not happen again; and he argued that the island was totally uninhabitable for a white man with a wife and children. People agreed with his suggestion, and a few weeks later Hrómundur and his family had moved to Spry Bay. And there he died a few years ago. His children received a good education, and one of his daughters married Dr. Patrick's eldest son.

And it was Donald, the giant Donald Gaskell, who often said that it was quite extraordinary how an old foreigner, who hardly spoke English, could have snatched a fully grown man out of the hands of a large group of Scotsmen and Irishmen in the prime of their lives and run away with him against his will in broad daylight.

"It was a man who did that, my boys," said Donald, "that was a *man!*"

Translated by Kirsten Wolf

ÁLFUR OF BORG

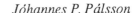

Jóhannes P. Pálsson

Jóhannes Páll Pálsson (1881-1973) was born in Reykjar at Reykjaströnd, Skagafjörður. He came to Canada in 1893 and settled in New Iceland. He was a school teacher for a while, and later studied medicine at the University of Manitoba. From 1909 he practised medicine in several Icelandic settlements in Canada. His writings include *Hnausaför mín* (Winnipeg, 1928) as well as several plays and short stories, which were published in *Lögberg, Heimskringla, Saga, Tímarit Þjóðræknisfélags Íslendinga*, and *Canadian Magazine*.

"Álfur of Borg" is translated from "Álfur á Borg" in *Saga* (1926-1927), pp. 161-172. The story was reprinted in Einar H. Kvaran and Guðm. Finnbogason, eds., *Vestan um haf* (Reykjavík, 1930), pp. 437-446.

1.

HELGI RESTED HIS ELBOWS on the desk and cradled his head in his hands. He had completely forgotten that the final exams would soon begin, that Caesar had fought the Gauls, and that an old Latin textbook lay on the desk in front of his nose. Helgi stared out the open window down on the street, or rather into vacancy. The hubbub and bustle of the city confused him; but the spring stretched its soft arm in through the window and caressed his cheeks and forehead. This was a true relief, to live in the maelstrom of life but not to let oneself be carried with the stream. To be a part of the game of life, but still be a spectator. To see life vibrate and pulsate in the street, and be equally fond of everything and everybody.

But something came into view that woke Helgi from this trance. He rubbed his eyes and watched a big, strong farmer, who had walked up and down the opposite side of the street studying the house numbers numerous times. Under his arm the man carried a long parcel tied with a string.

Álfur of Borg had arrived in the city. Impossible! But those shoulders – and the beard. It had to be him.

Helgi leapt to his feet, shot down the stairs and across the street like a bullet. "Álfur, Álfur. How are you, and welcome to the city."

"How are you, Helgi. It's good to see you. I was looking for the number of your house, but I was clearly on the wrong side of the street." Álfur smiled. When he smiled, his big, blue eyes brimmed with a joy that brightened up his whole face, right out to the cheekbones and all over his beard – out to his shoulders and down to his stomach. Then he stroked his beard and became serious. It was not a cloud that blocked out the sun; rather, the sun peeped out among the clouds. That was how Álfur smiled.

"Come along to my cubbyhole and tell me the news, dear fellow. How is everyone in Mörk? Where are you going? And what is in the parcel there?" The questions fell from Helgi's lips like shavings from the woodcutter's axe.

When they had come up to Helgi's room, Álfur looked around and placed the parcel against the wall in a corner. Helgi kept on asking questions, even though he got no answer. "Aren't you going to tell me any news?"

"Not if you keep asking questions like this. I'm not quick enough. It's the same with everybody and everything. Everyone is in a hurry, and even though you sit down for a second, you jabber away like a windmill in a westerly storm."

Helgi laughed.

"I've come to ask you a favour, Helgi. I must speak with a Canadian here in the city, but as you know, I don't speak English. Will you interpret for me?"

"Of course, I'd be delighted. I owe you more than that."

"I'm not so sure. And of course, I can do something for you in return."

"No, not at all. I haven't forgotten how good you and Þórunn were to me when I was a destitute immigrant. I'll certainly be your interpreter – that is, if you are not going to tell off the governor."

"No, but I must speak with a man who's probably more powerful than the governor."

Helgi felt uncomfortable. Álfur never joked. Moreover, he was known throughout the Mörk colony as an opinionated and somewhat odd fellow. He did not really take part in the social life of the colonists, and no election pollster had ever been able to persuade him from his convictions. The man was knowledgeable about genealogy and could trace his family back to Egill at Borg and was quite proud of being descended from such a famous man. In addition, he was married to an educated woman from one of the best families in Iceland. He had taken her from her home and disappeared with her to the western world. Helgi did not think that Álfur boasted about this, but he thought it likely that he firmly followed his intentions, whatever they might be. No, he was not to be trifled with.

"It's the president of the railway company with whom I have an errand," said Álfur stroking his beard.

"But what on earth makes you think that he'll listen to you or people like us when entire committees have to wait for days to seize a good opportunity to speak with him?"

"I'll tell you, my boy. This is probably the twelfth time that the weaklings from Mörk have sent a committee to ask for a railway line to the colony. They're now drifting about here in the city and have made an appointment with Þorbjörn tomorrow at two o'clock. We'll go in with the committee, and then I can get to speak with him."

"But surely Mr. Thorburn, or Þorbjörn as you call him, will throw us out."

Álfur looked firmly and calmly at Helgi, and stroked his beard.

"No he won't. I don't think he'll try."

"But what is your errand with Mr. Thorburn?"

"I want to recommend that he build a bit of railway line to the colony."

"And isn't that what the committee is going to propose?"

"Yes, and they'll probably do it in the same manner as before. Our MP will jabber away about the hard work of the colonists, the rich sources of water and timber, legitimate demands and other things that one can talk sixteen to the dozen about without coming up with a single useful idea. I assure you, my boy, that the leading figures of

Norse descent like Þorbjörn have long become fed up with this kind of farce. He doesn't take this kind of prattle any more seriously than does the moon when the dogs bark at it."

"But Mr. Thorburn is Scottish." Helgi couldn't let this happen. He had to bring Álfur to his senses.

"Yes, he's from the northern shores of Scotland. The Vikings landed there in ancient times and some of them settled there. His surname is a clear witness to his ancestry and origin. And it's likely that Norse Viking blood runs in the veins of a man who moved to another continent as a destitute youth and made his way to one of the most powerful positions in the country."

"But I always thought that you didn't care for a railway line to Mörk. And some of the colonists in Mörk bear a grudge against you for that reason."

"Oh, I don't care too much about the railway, my boy. But I find it sad that year after year our settlers should waste time and money trying to convince the leaders of this country that they are good-for-nothings and fools, who yearly kneel down in prayer before this Þorbjörn, take his ambiguous answer for an oracle, and are happy with anything. Someone has to put an end to this disgrace, and I want to try."

"Do you intend to get Mr. Thorburn to promise that the railway line will never be built?"

"Yes, that or the opposite, that he has it built soon. The younger men certainly need it. They don't consider themselves men anymore unless they can sit down to work, like old women at a washing tub, or make a quick trip into town."

Helgi had become depressed and distressed, and regretted having promised Álfur to interpret for him.

"You're probably ashamed to let Þorbjörn see you in my company, Helgi." There was a gentle touch of sadness in his voice. "But you probably wouldn't blush if you were on the committee. That's because you're still unable to appreciate the correct value of things. These members of the committee will appear tomorrow before Þorbjörn like fish out of water. Just wait and see. They'll wriggle like earthworms in their cheap Sunday clothes and consider it an honour to appear like beggars before the chieftain. Þorbjörn is a man like me, Helgi." And now Álfur spoke with determination. "He's been true to himself and has guarded the manliness that he inherited from his forefathers. He's never pretended to be anything other than what he is, and he's never let the lapping and barking of gossipers and rabble-rousers affect him. Don't you think I recognize the Norse character? Don't you think that Þorbjörn knows it?" The man was now on his feet, looking kindly at the youth, who blushed right to the tip of his ears. Álfur stood like that for a moment, still as the grave. To Helgi he could have been a stone monument or a rock. This frightful giant was equipped with some strange power. . . .

"What do you say, Helgi?"

It took Helgi a moment to find his bearings. "Yes, Álfur. I'll come with you to Þorbjörn. It's an honour for me, not a shame. And this is the first time in my life that I've been certain that it's good to be an Icelander." The youth's eyes became moist. But Álfur's eyes filled with joy, and his beard shone like a rough, open sea in the midnight sun.

2.

IT WAS ALMOST TWO O'CLOCK when the two fellows entered the waiting room: Helgi, an urban, slender, neat person; Álfur, big and impressive, respectably dressed in everyday clothes, with a long cylinder under his arm. He looked odd with that parcel, but Helgi had no say in that. Álfur had to have everything his way. They greeted the men from their own district who were sitting there – the members of the committee, dressed-up and polite. The Icelandic MP was there too, the self-elected chair of the committee. He frowned and asked the person sitting next to him if Álfur of Borg was on the committee. With that the door to Mr. Thorburn's office was opened, and his secretary asked the committee to enter. Álfur and Helgi withdrew but slipped in before the door was closed.

The MP introduced the members of the committee as soon as they entered. Mr. Thorburn greeted them with a handshake and was most pleasant. But when it was Álfur and Helgi's turn, the MP hesitated.

"How do you do," said Mr. Thorburn, and gave Álfur a firm handshake.

"How do you do, Þorbjörn," said Álfur in Icelandic.

"What did you say this giant's name was?" Mr. Thorburn asked the MP.

"This is Álfur of Borg," said Helgi. "He was greeting you in Icelandic."

The members of the committee shuddered.

"A damned scandal," thought the MP, but out loud he said, "he isn't a member of the committee. He's staying in the city and accompanying the people from his district."

"It's obvious that he's staying in the city," said Mr. Thorburn, and smiled. "But now I shall listen to your case."

Álfur strode to a corner and Helgi followed him. There they stood while the MP presented the concerns of the committee. Álfur stood like a stone monument leaning against his cylinder.

Helgi thought that Álfur had described the event quite well the day before, even though the man had never served on a railway committee. He was not stupid.

Mr. Thorburn listened to the MP with great interest, but his eyes often wandered to Álfur as he stood there in the corner of his office.

When the speaker had finished, there was a short silence. Then Mr. Thorburn rose from his seat. He praised the colonists for their proficiency, and the members of the committee for their initiative. He said that their demands were fair, and promised to present them to the executive board of the company. The company would surely give them serious consideration. The MP would receive a written response within a month. Then Mr. Thorburn opened the door.

"I want to have a few words with you, Þorbjörn," said Álfur, and stretched while Helgi translated his words into English.

The members of the committee hurried out. The damned man, to bring such shame upon the Icelanders.

"Wait a minute," said Mr. Thorburn, and looked towards Helgi. And then he said farewell to the members of the committee and the MP with a handshake, and locked the door.

Meanwhile Álfur had untied the string around the parcel, coiled it, and put it in his sweater pocket.

"Well," said Mr. Thorburn, and turned towards Helgi, "now the old man has the floor. Let him speak, and you interpret for me. I would like to offer you a seat, but this giant looks far from tired." Mr. Thorburn smiled. Helgi translated his words for Álfur.

Álfur opened the parcel and exposed a handwoven rug with a big bearskin in the middle; the edges and the corners were beautifully embroidered. Then Álfur said, "It was a custom of our ancestors, the chieftains, Þorbjörn, when they visited one another, to exchange gifts in memory of their meeting. And I ask you to accept this treasure in memory of the men and women of the Mörk colony. This skin is from a bear I myself killed, and I'm certain that you'll neither find a bullet-hole nor damage from a trap on it. My wife, Þórunn, wove the cloth and embroidered on it pictures of some of the events in the life of the colonists who are remembered by the older generation. Now I trust that you're noble enough, Þorbjörn, that you don't let me return with this parcel. I shall have it as a testimony of your magnanimity, which the common people would call modesty, that if you accept this gift, you'll be too great a man to give those who ask you with sincerity an ambiguous reply." Álfur was silent for a second, looked firmly at Mr. Thorburn, and then he said, "Is your company going to build a railway line to Mörk? And if so, when?"

Mr. Thorburn had been sitting quietly and seriously with his eyes focused on Álfur as he spoke. Now he stood up from his desk and went over to Álfur and Helgi. He took the rug from Álfur, studied it carefully, and then turned to Helgi.

"Tell this Nordic chieftain that I thank him for his visit. Tell him that it pleases me to see a Viking step out from the past, from over a thousand years ago, to meet with me. Tell him that I will visit him within two years and that I never travel a long distance except in a private railway coach. And tell him that I'll place this rug in front of my bed so that I won't forget my promise and that I thank him and his wife for the fine gift."

3.

LESS THAN TWO YEARS LATER there was a great celebration in Mörk. The long-awaited railway line had finally come to the colony. The town was still under construction, but a big hall had been found for the event. What made the celebration even more splendid was that Mr. Thorburn, president of the railway company, had arrived in a private coach and was, of course, the guest of honour. After him came the MP and then the members of the district council and old members of the railway committee.

Speeches were given at the table, most of them in praise of the zealous work of the colonists, the proficiency of the MP, and the virtues of Mr. Thorburn. The conservatism and strange views of those who didn't care about the progress of the colony were also referred to. People knew that they were alluding to Álfur of Borg and the likes of him and thought that it was well-deserved. Álfur was not at the banquet and was not missed until Mr. Thorburn asked for him. When he found out that Álfur was at home, he excused himself, hired a chauffeur, and drove to Borg.

Translated by Kirsten Wolf

HÁVARÐUR FROM KRÓKUR

Kveldúlfur

The identity of the author writing under the pseudonym Kveldúlfur (Evening Wolf) remains unknown, and no other works have appeared under this name.

"Hávarður from Krókur" is translated from "Hávarður úr Króki" in *Voröld* 2 March 1920, pp. 2-3. The story was reprinted in Einar H. Kvaran and Guðm. Finnbogason, eds., *Vestan um haf* (Reykjavík, 1930), pp. 546-551.

THE EVENING SUN was setting behind the leafless bushes to the west of the plains. Pale, chilly rays slipped in through the window and shone with a dim evening light on the bald spot and the thin, almost white, hair of old Hávarður from Krókur. Old Hávarður sat at his desk by the window watching some noisy boys who amused themselves by throwing small stones at an old cat, which, mewing, fled behind the garden gate.

"The last scene of the play," the old man grumbled resentfully, and began to read under his breath a newly written letter that was lying on the desk.

In about an hour I'll be stone dead. That's for sure. This morning I woke up with a damned headache just like some years ago, the day I had the stroke, and then again five years ago, when I had the same attack. Yes, I'm definitely out of the story. My old body can hardly take anything these days, and besides, I've lost all desire to live and the will to fight against death. Earlier I felt that I must not possibly die. First I wanted power and esteem, and then later, when that failed to come about, I hoped for at least a little recognition, to see some little result of my life's work, because, to be honest, I haven't been idle. But am I then not content to go? Have I then been defeated? Oh no, I win a victory now, in death. Just take notice of what the papers will say tomorrow. Do you perhaps think they'll call me a rebel, a traitor, or something like that, when I am dead? No,

69

believe me, they'll change their tune, because then it won't be called treason if people agree with my views. And believe me, my views have taken root among the people. But that was not to be mentioned, because then I might become a dangerous rival to the powers that be; then I would be an obvious leader, of course. But the nation can't stand still, the human mind can't be fettered for long; it must break its bonds, or else die. And the bonds are a legacy of past times; all that we call "customs, laws or obedience" are just old clothing that mankind tailored to suit its own interests, according to its development and situation. But mankind develops and changes, and the old clothes, the old arrangements, become worn and outdated, and new clothing must be tailored.

But the pioneers, the light-bearers, what becomes of them? Alive they are persecuted; but dead they are made saints. Their labour is wasted; their vital force is wasted like the drop that hollows the rock, or the ray of sunshine that struggles to melt the ice until it itself becomes cold and dies. Yes, they are wasted, but not for nothing, because the rock is cleft and the ice is melted.

You see that I'm now becoming poetic, but that must be forgiven at the hour of death.

Apart from that, I want to ask you to look after Dísa when I'm gone. I sent her almost against her will to the bath house on the beach this morning, because I wished to spare her the worst by not being at home.

Well, you must forgive me for not coming next autumn to go duck shooting with you, because, as you see, it'll be impossible for me. Farewell.

Yours ever, Hávarður from Krókur."

He folded the letter and addressed it very calmly with a steady hand: "To the Honourable Sheriff in Austursýsla." Then he carefully put it away and started looking at two pictures that hung on the wall. One was of a serious, grey-haired woman in black clothes. That was his mother, who had rocked him to sleep and read to him beautiful prayers in the evenings when he was a child. Would he now get to see her again there on the other side? The other was of Dísa – pretty, in a white summer dress, just like she was at the bonfire, when he gave Long Jói a black eye for walking her home in the evening. That summer he drank black tea and ate dry bread in order to be able to ask her to the students' banquet in the winter. "I think I'll never be able to repay you for this," she'd said when she found out. Never be able to repay him? Hadn't she repaid him many times? Because it was after all she who had made him a happy man. The worst thing was that he couldn't take her with him. Because no matter what it would be like on the other side, he would still be sad if he had to wait a long time for her – and she would feel no better than he.

The light slowly disappeared in the living room, and then night came.

There were flags at half-mast all over the city, and people with worried looks everywhere. "What's happened?" asked those who did not know. "Hávarður from Krókur, the leader of the liberals, has died," the others answered with emotion.

The gravity was, however, greatest in Parliament, where his seat was draped in black.

"What's going to happen?" the pompous, fat MPs thought, whom people had elected merely because thy were "steady" and likely to stand like rocks in the way of all risky changes and put a stop to this terrible man and his revolutionary followers, who, the papers said, would lead everything – both the nation and the people – to hell, if he came to power. They had made up slander about him and his followers a long time ago, which they used in all elections; but now, of course, it was of no use any longer, because the man was dead. So now they had to resort to something else, and God knows how they would manage with a new topic to speak about. Never had they found their seats as soft as right now, but soon there would be elections, and then everything about the future would be uncertain. As one would expect, the greatest look of worry was on the prime minister.

"Yes, now the damned idiots will turn him into a saint, and the papers praise him." Oh, how despicable, how foolishly loathsome to have offended the man and degraded him while he was alive and could feel it, and then to have to praise him immediately after he had died. But people were so unspeakably stupid. Ah well, he need not carp about it, even though it was a bit silly. It might come in handy, if only one knew how to play on the crazy feelings that undeniably prevail in most people. But that could also be damned hard. Enough of that. Something had to be done. The worst thing was that he was struggling with himself, a struggle against the antipathy, the nauseating disgust with all this absurd farce that both he and probably all other intellectual men constantly have to play in order to please the masses. At times he literally hated himself for having turned into this farcical monster. And the desire – the instinctive desire of his own half-dead human nature – told him to drop the mask and have the courage of his own convictions. Again and again he had almost given way to this silly desire, this terrible weakness, as he himself called it. But what kind of stupidity was this? Should he perhaps pull the rug from under his feet? Should he perhaps risk his future just in order to comply with these damned whims? No, now he must be rational, now he had to play it right.

He was on his feet to give his speech. Everyone was silent. "I probably need not describe to the honourable members of Parliament what a loss we and the nation have suffered through this death. Although we did not always agree on certain issues, we had many things in common, such as the love of the fatherland and the sincere will to be loyal to it. Now that death's cold hand has separated us from earthly association, we are certainly closer to each other in sympathetic understanding. So it will be at least for our great and noble colleague, who has now been reborn to a higher understanding in another and better life; and so it will also be for us, even though we are still subordinate to the frailty and shortsightedness of earthly existence. Isn't it an irrefutable witness to man's divine nature that he can forgive everything in death? Now, at this very solemn moment, when death has cut a new gap in the circle of friends and thus reminded us of the reality of death and eternity, of the absolute promise and eternal bliss, where human frailty disappears like a mote of dust, we want to try and forget unpleasant memories and remember only that which, in spite of everything, may have taken place that was always innermost and deepest in the consciousness of all of us who have borne the burden and heat of the day, united in the spirit of common responsibility and common love of our nation and our people. In order that we, colleagues and friends of the deceased, show our obvious and appropriate grief and sympathy for the death of this noble and true son of the fatherland, I wish to make the proposal that the government and the Parliament express their sincere condolences to the bereaved widow and family."

The prime minister waited while the proposal was unanimously adopted. Then he continued, "To show the memory of the deceased due respect, I further propose that the meeting be adjourned indefinitely."

With that the MPs leaped to their feet – they had almost forgotten their grand airs and official looks – and hurried away like exuberant boys from school.

The ceremony was festive. The most magnificent church in the capital was packed with people. A solemn dirge resounded high in the vaulted nave. A black coffin, covered with beautiful wreaths, stood before the altar. The most distinguished priests of the city and the nation's best orators vied with each other in their praise of Hávarður from Krókur, who was now unfortunately dead and unable to enjoy it. The prime minister spoke best, however, and when he emotionally spoke of "the eternal atonement," most were moved, and some even shed tears.

The funeral procession went to the graveyard. Six MPs walked respectfully behind the hearse in honour of the deceased.

The coffin descended into the grave. Lumps of earth fell with a thud on the lid, but the clatter of the half-frozen soil was almost drowned by the wailing of the hymns. Some of the more distinguished men formed a dignified circle around the grave with a sorrowful look, which they guarded carefully. They would not even admit it to themselves that in their hearts they were just a little bit glad, because it was undeniably lucky to be able to bury old Hávarður from Krókur just before the elections.

Translated by Kirsten Wolf

MOTES IN A SUN-BEAM

Stephan G. Stephansson

Stephan G. Stephansson (1853-1927) was born at Kirkjuhóll, Skagafjörður. In 1873, he emigrated with his parents to the United States. He was three times a pioneer, first in Wisconsin in 1874; then in North Dakota in 1880; and lastly in Markerville, Alberta, in 1889, where he lived as a farmer for the rest of his life.

Despite the hard toil of pioneer farm-life Stephan G. Stephansson was a prolific writer. And he is the most acclaimed of the immigrant writers by critics both in the East and the West. Stefán Einarsson (*History of Icelandic Prose Writers 1800-1940,* Islandica 32-33, Ithaca, 1948) calls him "the greatest American-Icelandic writer" (p. 243), Watson Kirkconnell (in *University of Toronto Quarterly* 5 [1935-1936], pp. 263-277) argues that he is "Canada's leading poet" (p. 263), and F. Stanton Cawley (in *Scandinavian Studies and Notes* 15 [1938], pp. 99-109) claims that he is "the greatest poet of the Western World" (p. 99). His poems and essays, many of which appeared in Western Icelandic newspapers and periodicals, were later published in the collections *Úti á víðavangi* (Winnipeg, 1894), *Á ferð og flugi* (Reykjavík, 1900), *Andvökur* I-VI (Reykjavík and Winnipeg, 1909-38), *Kolbeinslag* (Winnipeg, 1914), *Heimleiðis* (Reykjavík, 1917), *Vigslóði* (Reykjavík, 1920), *Jökulgöngur* (Wynyard,1921), *Andvökur. Úrval* (Reykjavík, 1939), *Úrvalsljóð* (Reykjavík, 1945), *Gullregn úr ljóðum Stephans G. Stephanssonar* (Reykjavík, 1967), *Bréf og ritgerðir* I-IV (Reykjavík, 1938-48), and *Frá einu ári. Kvæði, bréf og erindi frá árinu 1891* (Reykjavík, 1970).

Though chiefly a lyric poet, Stephan G. Stephansson also wrote a number of short stories. During the years between 1894 and 1901, he wrote a series of sketches called "Ar" ("Motes in a Sun-Beam"). These sketches – "Buried Alive," "The Morning Breeze," "Greybeard," "Charity and Fairness," "Foreboding," "The Last Plover," "The Death of Old Guðmundur the Student," "The New Hat," and "The Seventh Day" – are translated from "Kviksettur," "Morgunvindurinn," "Gráskeggur," "Kærleikur og Sanngirni,"

"Fyrirför," "Seinasta lóan," "Fráfall Guðmundar gamla stúdents," "Nýi hatturinn" and "Sjöundi dagurinn" in *Heimskringla* 1894-1901. Five of these sketches ("The Morning Breeze," "Greybeard," "Foreboding," "The Last Plover" and "The Death of Old Guðmundur the Student") were reprinted in Einar H. Kvaran and Guðm. Finnbogason, eds., *Vestan um haf* (Reykjavík, 1930), pp. 552-572. All nine sketches were published in *Bréf og ritgerðir* IV, pp. 41-76.

---

1. Buried Alive

NOW AND THEN you've urged me to recite for you a verse, dear children. If you think that I did it to please you, I must be straight with you. I merely recite verses in order not to have to listen to you, so that your yelling doesn't drive me crazy. You've long been displeased with me, because my poems are about clouds and woods and other such incomprehensible and indigestible things, and because I've never bothered to recite hymns or flattering verses about you, nor panegyrics about Titus Tallowshield of whom you are so fond because he pretends to be the son of a rich man. You've not been particularly interested in my epics, because no one's skull has been cleaved nor has anyone's heart been pierced, for if any of my heroes have felt a bit of pain, although caused by people, it was nonetheless always by what you call accidents, and not with spears and bullets. And your brains and hearts are still so small that one needs binoculars to see them, as you might say. I hope they grow, grow a lot, later – and then . . .

No, I shall make no guesses. But now I intend to be entertaining and compose in the way I expect you to like best. I shall write about the things you all believe in, that this world is nothing but a large soup bowl around which we're all sitting, and that the happiest is the one who snatches the most and the fattest bits; and to console the ones who get nothing or who sit with thin soup, I shall compose as poignantly as I can verses relating that above us all hangs an even larger soup bowl, where one day everyone will get more, and more than enough, and no one will be excluded. In addition, I intend to place distinguishing numbers on the clouds, so that you know which one I'm writing about each time, and then my poems will be approximately as follows, with regard to title and content.

Poem about the black cloud number two, which sits on the ridge of Skollakollur:

The rain will come from it, I think,
so that the dry earth moist grows.
Our cows will then be in the pink,
and from them delicious cream flows.

Perhaps it's not possible to sing this verse, although it is a tetrameter;
but I hope I'll improve so that eventually I'll be able to compose
octametric hymns like the ones you learn in Sunday school, dear
children.

But it just so happens that today I don't feel like composing. I'm
like a fiddle that has been stored in a damp place – I've lost my tune.
Therefore, I want to tell you a story, but it's not about me, rather, it's
a story about a man who was buried alive. I hope you'll understand it,
especially those of you who fear more than anything to end up being
buried alive.

Everywhere, on streets and stairs, in towns and houses, he met
them, these miserable dwarfs, with bony hands and bent backs, with
downcast countenances and misty eyes. He felt sorry for them and
asked who had hurt them and stopped their growth. They all told the
same story, and they all told it in the same way. They took him to a
private place, where they thought no one would see them or hear
them, stretched up to his ears, cupped their hands around the words,
so that they streamed straight into his ear, and were not whispered to
the public out of the side of the mouth that turned away from him.

"Our hands have become bony from all the hard work, especially
over the last years, for us to have food to eat sometimes and towards
a pension for Capitalist, our bankrupt merchant and his family, who
in ten years became so wealthy that he'll never have to work again,
although he's not even forty years old. Our backs have become bent
from carrying the burden of taxes, which the government places upon
us, for raising horses for fun and for riding, while using us as
packhorses. And we have such downcast countenances, because
Reverend Steinn and the Church have threatened to call us heathens
and villains, if we don't humbly believe that our children, on whom
the government takes revenge by hanging them for what it calls a
serious crime, are still tortured in hell, on the other side of the gallows
and the grave mound. But we've never been able to believe that about
our own children, although we consider it likely about the children of

77

Unitarians. God help us! We've had to brood on this but never dared to say it aloud, because we want to have priests and churches, and not to become fools and villains, but instead be Christians like we are. The misty cloud over our eyes is from staring. From as far back as we can remember, we were not allowed to look away from these three things: faith, law and custom. Those in power imprisoned all who deviated from these. Now and then they executed them, but for us, who were obedient and helpful, they held a punishment-celebration to keep us going."

Then he asked them if they were pleased with these conditions, and if they desired any changes.

"Yes, in God's name, in God's name," they shouted, those who writhed with hunger. "In the name of fairness," others interrupted, and rubbed their bony hands. "In the name of humanity and brotherhood," some mumbled and hung their heads imploringly. "In the name of reason and progress," others quickly added, and rubbed their eyes. "In the name of freedom," they shouted with one voice. "We'd reward him well who'd set us free."

On Monday he wrote in his paper, *Frankness*, an article about how the property of destitute people was tricked away from them. He tried to demonstrate that under the present financial laws of so-called civilized people, poor people paid the highest taxes, and that reliable people had to pay indirectly the debts of the dishonest. He also pointed out that the ones who owned nothing but made a living from toil alone, paid taxes to others on all necessities in this country, where all goods were taxed, because he could not grant himself anything, and that through trickery in sales and purchases, slyness had made them provide sufficiently for itself by estimating ten to twenty-five percent of the price of many popular goods as money lost into the hands of stupid and dishonest debtors, and the smaller merchants then followed the same rule. Therefore, they increased the price for those who paid, about ten or twenty-five percent in order to avoid losses, and as a consequence they were twenty-five times wealthier. He referred to Capitalist, the bankrupt merchant, whom all knew began from nothing and went bankrupt with enormous debts, which he never paid, and whom all knew now to be an idle, wealthy man. Such men, he said, were in reality worse than arrant thieves.

The day after Capitalist had read the article about himself, he was highest on the collection list with a $100 gift to the famine-fund, so that the hungriest got a free meal each day, while the outburst of compassion among the rich people was hottest and the bad weather of Providence coldest. When this had become known and when the crowd of those with bony hands and misty eyes met the bankrupt merchant in the street, they moved aside for him and bowed grate-fully, as those who are doomed bow before a guardian spirit. Those who themselves had always shirked their work, when the foreman looked away, found that it was a unique, meritorious conscientious-ness that once in a while voluntarily paid human society one millionth of the interest on capital which it had unlawfully acquired.

On Tuesday his paper included an article about highwaymen in politics. In this article he attempted to demonstrate that in no other country were half the taxes paid by the citizens used for general necessities. Paupers were called "welfare cases," and that was consid-ered a degrading word. "Political paupers" were called "government officers," because people had agreed that it was a title of honour. This often constituted the whole difference among people. He used their government as an example of the manner in which expenditure was decided upon, and mentioned some political welfare cases by name, such as Error Backpack, who was sent all over the country with an empty government bag in his possession, with the sole purpose of giving governmental pretence to his $3,000 annual salary. He con-cluded by saying that their so-called liberal government was in reality a gang of robbers and tyrants.

The next day Error Backpack carried around a petition for signatures, declaring that the government should cease giving funds to road repairs and water culverts for the bogs in the remote settle-ment, Heath Thing; the taxes were too high for the general public, because of the costs involved. Those with bent backs and downcast countenances all wanted to sign their names, and the most keen were the ones who could not write their name themselves but had to get others to do it for them. They themselves lived in cities with paved roads and didn't give a damn if their fellow countrymen in Heath Thing were stuck in the bogs out there. It was too much to expect them to pay to help drag them out of the bogs; they could do that themselves. In the evening they added a new redeemer to their faith: Error. He was after all the only progressive man who would do something to the advantage of the general public. How could they reproach him for accepting what was handed to him by the government charlatans and not refusing what they knew he did not work for – they who themselves were never satisfied with life, because they so rarely got something for nothing, merely because they had been slighted by Providence in getting their share of craftiness or because they had not been sent to school in their youth.

On Wednesday his latest essay came out, about spiritual financial tricks. He said that the Church and the schools were partners in extinguishing and hiding any spiritual spark among the common people, which, they feared, could light up and become a fire. They tried to tread it down in the ashes of burned-out figments of the imagination, under the heavy arrogance of scholarship and words of contempt. While this took place, there was little light and warmth, and therefore the earth was crawling with all kinds of spiritual cripples, of whom sincerity, strength of thought, and noble-mindedness had been squeezed out. He considered it likely that many teachers like, for example, Reverend Steinn Parrot, taught the way they did, merely because the Church, which they served, was stronger than their own convictions; they dared not change anything, because that would be to pull down the house over their own heads. He concluded by saying that such people were seated at tables with popes and hypocrites.

In the evening there was a meeting of the congregation in Reverend Steinn's chapel. To pass the time those with bony hands and bent backs, with downcast countenances and misty eyes, showed up. They wanted more than anything to be called Christians. It was explained to them that they could continue to keep that name unchallenged, although they did not believe some of the things they had been taught, as long as they did not mention it aloud in the same way as their first Christian ancestors were allowed to expose their children – as long as they did it in secret. The priest encouraged them to practise concealing their opinions. Those with bony hands and misty eyes welcomed this change; it suited them so well. They could not imagine a more perfect man of God than Reverend Steinn nor a man more liberal. They did not find it offensive, although he did it to retain his peaceful life and his honourable position, to permit people to doubt in secret the truth of what he himself taught them; nor was it to be expected that he taught what he believed in. They knew that there was only a very slight difference between his dishonesty and theirs – they who were all bought on the last election day for an insignificant honorarium to vote for the policy of a minister, which they suspected was worse.

He came to them on Thursday where they were loafing about at their workplace, happier and prouder than usual, because now "the biggies" had been defeated. "Now I have to rely on your honour, good brothers," he said. "I think I can find refuge here. I've supported your case to the best of my ability, though little has as yet been accomplished. Perhaps we'll achieve more later if we stick together. But as a result the ones in power hate me, and according to the laws of this country anyone who is thus hated and is poor and supports himself by manual work must be buried alive. These laws do not apply to wealthy people. I need money to save my skin. There are many of you, my brothers, and I've spoken our common cause. Can you help me?"

"Help you with money, give you money? No, never. We're hard up even without you. Supported our cause! Yes, we'll believe that! If you've done anything in that direction, it's been in your own interest, to get at your enemies and scold them, but we don't get involved if you and your enemies quarrel. We don't scold anyone publicly, and you'll have to be responsible for your actions. You've called a generous man an arrant thief, a friend of the public a tyrant, and a liberal priest a hypocrite. No, this can't be salvaged. We don't need your words any more. What we didn't like is now being corrected. Moreover, we've got no money."

He clenched his teeth while they spoke, held his breath, and kept each nerve in his face still as the grave, like when people pull themselves together to do something they find disgusting, such as pushing away a dead snake. There were no more emotions in his voice when he answered them than in the voice of a prisoner who had heard his death sentence, which he knew from the beginning he would get, but who was kept waiting until he had become tired of being in prison.

"It's a misunderstanding that I've scolded people in my fury, but like lightning, truth doesn't make a detour, and if you find the air cleaner and easier to breathe than before, it's because of that. Let's not talk about merits or sympathy, let's simply say that it's my nature, or fate, to advocate the cause of wretched people. I trust that it's in accordance with your kind heart to save a person who is to be buried alive. It's more painful than being hanged. What is your daily salary now?"

"We recently got a raise to two dollars, at long last. But if you can raise the salary about fifty cents, then we'll give you our raise on the first day."

"No, there's no way of doing that today. Tomorrow is Friday, and then I am to be buried alive. I only asked to point out that one day's salary could save me."

"One day's salary for all of us? We'd starve to death if we lost that. No, never, never." He left them without any success.

On Friday morning when those with bony hands and bent backs, with downcast countenances and misty eyes, went to work, someone said, "Today is the day of his burial."

"His burial! Yes, I'd forgotten all about it."

"I've never seen a man being buried alive."

"It's probably weird. Shouldn't we go and have a look?"

"But we may lose our jobs and salaries."

"Never mind, we have so few days off. We can't miss an entertainment; we have so few of them."

"Let's go."

They all took the day off to see what it was like to be buried alive.

Translated by Kirsten Wolf

2. The Morning Breeze

"BEAUTIFUL LIKE THE SUMMER and glorious like the sun," sang the morning breeze, as he rushed down the hill of beauty. All the roses on the hill looked up, stared after him and blushed. "Whom do you think he meant?" "Which one of us do you think he spoke of?" they whispered as they put their heads together. It was the rustle of the grass. "Whom do you think he meant, then!" whistled an old tree on the next knoll. She was both older and able to see farther afield than the roses. "He certainly didn't mean any of you, you little fools. The morning breeze travels all over the wide, wide world and sees all its grandeur. He cares only about the most beautiful colour in that sunbeam and the prettiest bud on the willow there. He flies over land and sea searching for beauty. That's what he's singing about. Listen, he sings the same to the withered grass out on the marshes. Whom do you think he means!"

The morning breeze came again around noon. This was a land where the sun never sets in the spring, and therefore everything was rightfully named after the father of light, the morning. He sang the same tune; but this time the roses on the hill didn't look up. What pleasure would they derive from it if they were not allowed to imagine that the song was about them. They had started to wither. "You were brutal," said the morning breeze to the old tree, grabbing her hairy branches and bowing them down to the ground. "The hill, who believed what you said, is now fading away; but the marshes, who didn't hear you, are raptly turning green. Didn't you know that it's a crime to wipe away contentment and the sense of beauty, even with the truth?"

Translated by Árný Hjaltadóttir

3. Greybeard

IN THE EVENING, a man called Greybeard walked into the tent before King Útsteinn; and when they had greeted each other, the king looked at him and asked, "Where were you born? Who are your parents, and what skills do you possess, old man? From what country did you come, and what is your business here? What have you seen on your journeys, for you must have travelled far, or where are you heading?"

"Sir, you ask many questions," answered Greybeard, "and I don't know if I can answer them. My parents were peasants; and I have thus traced my genealogy far enough, for no learning is more contrary to the truth than genealogy. My native country is Land, because Air and

Sea always lead me astray. My only skill is my ability to appear as the one I am. I came from Whiteman's country, and I've finished my business there, because I've searched for prosperity and found it. I'm now on my way homewards; as yet, I don't know the direction, but I've only a short distance to travel. I don't know of any more adventures."

"Tell us more fully about your findings," said Útsteinn. "We and our court are also on such a journey and have thus far failed to accomplish our mission."

"Turn back, King," answered Greybeard. "The one you seek led you astray and then went back home. But I was still young, when I joined Queen Amenity, and for a while I enjoyed her service. To her I gave my innocence and other costly things and gained experience; but I wasn't content there for long, because she wanted earnestness. Then I went to the earl of Pride; to him I brought modesty and received knowledge of human nature, but he wanted also justice and that caused our separation. Next I stayed with the king of Wealth. I gave him generosity, but he gave me practicality in return. I left that place because he wanted to lure honesty from me. Then I thought that I had taxed those chieftains sufficiently, and so visited wise men. First I entered a monastery with Abbot Piety. He forced me to give up worship but sold me idealism. I ran away from him because he wanted to rob me of reason. From there I went to Professor Sage. I brought him confidence and accepted knowledge from him, but I couldn't stay there very long, because he wanted to take my imagination as well. For a while I stayed with the poet Bragi. He took all I owned, and in return I gained the sense of beauty, but I ran away long ago, because food was often scarce."

Then King Útsteinn said, "You have ranged widely, but small are your accomplishments."

"My story is not yet finished," answered Greybeard. "I felt I had no refuge anywhere, and that my hopes had become fickle. Then I looked at my own nature and there, King, I found prosperity. I had carried it heedlessly within my heart throughout the whole journey."

"Now you tell a great lie," answered Útsteinn, "because I can tell from your appearance, your old age and weariness that wretched is the one who has been driven about as a beggar."

"Sir, prosperity isn't recognized by appearances or occupation," said Greybeard. "Rather, it is found in courage, which doesn't recognize, neither in life nor in death, a force greater than its own, and in a mind that gains its reward from its own achievements. King, as I have already advised you, turn back!"

"Old man, we don't believe your story," answered the king, "and we will look farther, before we return home."

"I knew your answer beforehand," said Greybeard. "We must all travel the same road and must search far before we find prosperity. Outwards lies our path, and yet it is always inwards. But few manage to find the way home again."

That night Greybeard disappeared from the tent, and no one knew where he had gone. Some thought that he had been Odin or some such supernatural being.

Translated by Árný Hjaltadóttir

4. Charity and Fairness

CENTURY AFTER CENTURY and year after year they had been travelling companions throughout the world. They were old when the first Christmas celebration was held on earth.

Nonetheless, they have never been able to lodge in the same place. Where Charity is welcomed, Fairness is denied shelter. In the hovel, where the door is opened unto Fairness, Charity cannot get a foot over the threshold.

Charity is friendly and smiling, like a respectable, upright man, with crosses and badges on his chest, like those who associate with bishops and kings.

Fairness is thoughtful and serious like a prophet in his own land and plainly dressed like a poor woman.

Charity is aristocratic, like one who is used to being in high rank. Fairness stoops like one who is used to waiting for a long time. This is how it is with Charity and Fairness.

All year they had been travelling about performing their task. On Christmas Eve the whole world is their destination.

From the newborn baby in the shed in Crime Street, Fairness

rushed to the nobleman's castle, where the heir was being swaddled. "This is shortsighted," she shouted, "this is shortsighted! Two generations useless for the nation. Poverty there and wealth here. Create equality between people! Then everyone will feel better." The servants pushed her outside the gate. They thought she had escaped from the lunatic asylum.

Before the gate shut, Charity came. The guards led him in with their hats in their hands. "There are no clothes for the child in Crime Street," said Charity. "No clothes. My God!" said the noblewoman. "Maid, give him some Christmas clothes." "I'll bring them myself," said Charity. Everyone bowed with respect as he was led down the stairs. Charity was not allowed to enter the shed in Crime Street, because he came from the nobleman's hall. Baseness and Wretchedness lived on his property and remembered that they had been unable to pay the rent. He turned away and instructed a heavily armed policeman to deliver the gifts.

Considerate people praised Charity to the skies. Then Fairness came to a court, where a sentence was being passed on a burglar who had killed a swindler for money. "Stop it," she screamed. "It's merely loss of blood and not an improvement to attempt to condemn half of the crime. Don't make wealth desirable, and release both the usurer and the murderer!" She was thrown out for contempt of court.

Charity came and reduced the sentence to life-long imprisonment. And good people admired Charity.

Fairness was present where Idleness stood with empty hands. "You're a bum," she said, "you, who live off other people's toil. An honest life is toil. Forget about all personal privileges that are handed down to you for such a life of idleness. Service alone is worthy of idle pastime, so that she may enjoy some of her own efforts." She was exiled because of her revolutionary theory.

Then came Charity with a bag of bread. It contained crumbs from full idle people to hungry idle people.

Charitable organizations fell on their knees before Charity.

Fairness came to where Ingenuity and Intelligence lived in resentment and negligence, because society chained them to the same bench as it did to counter-jumpers. "That's because noble-mindedness has been trampled down," she said. "Don't bury such powers alive;

place them where they may do justice to themselves, and don't squeeze out of them each honest drop of blood." She got a bad reputation for having robbed Craftiness of his cause.

With Charity's help they picked up good Christmas food as a reward for how witty and entertaining they could be at parties.

The liberals made Charity's name their war cry.

Fairness also came to where a great power was attempting to subdue its tributary country with the sword. "Let these people go in peace," she said to the great power. "It's better to have a contented friend than a subdued thrall, who does damage to both by being kept under control." She was threatened with treason.

Charity came when the war was over, when fathers had fallen and homes had been burnt. He collected money for widows and stood for political reform for the improvement of conditions for children and elderly people.

And the great poets composed hymns in honour of Charity, and the small poets composed four-lined stanzas.

Even the poets!

On Christmas Eve they met at the archbishop's gate. "Where are you going now?" asked Fairness.

"First I'm going in here," answered Charity, "then to the king, the headmaster, and the court poet. They have all invited me. Where are you going to spend the night?" He smiled sympathetically, like one who has accomplished much. "I don't know," replied Fairness, "I've not been invited anywhere."

She hurried down the icy, windy street. The cold wind led her like a companion. Up among the house ridges, a long and narrow fringe of grey, dry sky could be seen, with staring stars that were hardly visible, like the eyes of a man who sleeps with his eyes open. On both sides rimy rows of houses towered, with dark-grey smoke rising like poles from the chimneys, and with gleams of light shining from each window like a sparkling glacier. Nowhere did she ask for shelter for the night. She knew that each house was full of Christmas guests and that she was superfluous. Finally, she stopped by the smallest hut, farthest out in the poorest area of the city. The door was open, so that the light from the stars shone in and the smoke blew out. Inside, a faint shine came from the embers in an old boiler, like twigs scorching in a charcoal stack. It was the stove and the Christmas light. By the stove sat an old and exiled anarchist. He made a living selling matchsticks to cooks. In appearance he was grey and distorted like indignation itself and disgruntled like a bad conscience.

"Don't enter my house," he shouted. "You who steal the annual supply, but pretend to give a mouthful – away with your alms. You are the eighteenth I chase away tonight. Leave me alone!"

"I come to ask for a Christmas gift, not to give you one," said Fairness. "My name is Fairness. No one will put me up; all the houses are crowded, because everyone has invited Charity. Will you let me stay?"

"Welcome, poor wretch," answered the anarchist, "we can take turns sitting by the embers and sleeping in the chip pile."

Translated by Kirsten Wolf

5. Foreboding

"SOMETIMES I'M AFRAID OF HIM, when the expression on his face becomes unsettled like that of a criminal."

"That's how you remembered me, Miss Angel-Adviser. You dressed for the dance and thrust your snow-white hand into your glove."

"Unfortunately, you would never suspect this to be your fault. Yet, you remind me of him – like the victory march of the general through the city reminds me of the heaps of slain men that bridged the dyke outside the city."

"We could never be without him when we played. He was so clever and joyful. He worked for his own upbringing during the day and for our entertainment at night. Although he was tired and didn't want to do so, he could never say no."

"Have it your way," Consequence said to him. "Borrow from life, young man. I'll keep score. You're still so strong and healthy that you've only lost five years of your life," she said to him when he was just past twenty.

He smiled at her. Five years of old-age a long, long way off, of what use were they? And then it could have been miscalculated; it was definitely based on uncertainty.

He toiled all day until dark, and until every nerve in his body burned. At night he read and meditated until his eyes blurred and the arrival of dawn and the thought of rising tormented him.

"Now the difference is greater," said Consequence, when he was just over thirty. "You've lost ten years of your life, and that is a rather loose count."

It went in one ear and out the other. He based longevity on prominence, not years.

We anticipated that Consequence told the truth, but it was his willfulness that prevailed. He could eat well during the day and sleep soundly during the night like animals and many other able men.

He was busy from dawn until dark. In the evenings, when his anxieties had settled, speculations arose and kept him awake. It was the time of year when spring seeding was finished, but when one's own creativity begins to bud. He kept vigil and worked until he was no longer rejuvenated by spring nor revived even when he read a beautiful thought. Every feeling was dulled, except one – that all his life he had been shortening his life span.

"Fifteen years of operational losses," said Consequence.

"Now you must come to me," commanded Death.

Then we carried him to the grave, and all of us harboured the same thought – what a grievous folly it was to empty one's self to the last drop of blood, half a lifetime before one's time had come.

I know it was his own fault and that I am no more to blame than you and Cain. Yet sometimes, when I think about him, I become obsessed with a kind of anxiety that is related to the anguish of a soul suspicious of having committed a crime. Am I not a part of the soil from which the vegetation grows and which the sun scorches at such an early stage?

It is in those insane moments that you are afraid of my face, Miss Angel-Adviser.

Translated by Árný Hjaltadóttir

6. The Last Plover

ON THE SIDE OF THE VALLEY opposite me was a steep hill with screes and loose stones that had rolled down onto the crag by the canyon. No trail lay over the rough, stony ground. All vegetation had tumbled down to its death. On the side where I stood, the smooth sloping mountain with small fields and heathery moors on the broad promontory over by the hill wound itself, as if it felt sorry for the hill and had tried to grasp it with its hand giving it a warmer apparel. But the river rolled forth in between them with pitch-black pools and swift, clay-brown currents down into the abrupt crag sump and into the district, over the gravel bank and into the larger river. It was tired of the narrow passage in the glen and rushed to get into the mainstream of life and the wide world. It was a youth, not yet twenty years old, that tumbled into the larger river and got lost.

The weather was unusually good the whole month of September. It was as if the Icelandic autumn wanted the migrating plovers to remember it with kindness this time. Now they had all left. Then October arrived, the first part with an easterly snow storm and the second with a northerly frost. The third part of October was accompanied by a shifting southerly breeze and a clear sky. All things breathed iciness, and going outside was like stepping into a slushy bath. Wet snow covered the heath, except where it had melted. Here and there the crowberry heath poked its brown tipped branches out of the snow. Brooks and bogs were covered with ice and slush. The appearance of the cape had changed. Now it was like a beautiful soft hand, which one stroked in one's youth, before old age and weariness had knotted all the veins and pinched the nerves. The daylight was murky, like nightfall. The calm, cold weather trailed over the mouth of the valley and over the slopes. Due south the clouds broke, showing the rayless sun, which looked phosphorescent in the dusky pine forest; yet it seemed so near, as if it were hanging between the glacier and the bottom of the valley. Closer, in the deepest part of the valley, two light, golden shields glittered at the bottom of the grey snow coffin. There the river spread out along the flat sand banks, and the sun had stolen down there somehow, like the beautiful memories from one's youth.

"Hu, hu, hu," resounded in the heath above me, but the voice was toneless, like a wet fiddle string. It was the sound of the last plover, singing. Then the singing died when it could no longer sound the tune to deereedee.

Why had it not flown away with its companions? Why had it waited for the cold, snowy weather, the poor devil? Had it waited for dotage, because it thought in the cold, snowy weather of autumn that it could sing in its broken voice as sweetly as last spring, when it was young and expected the summer to last forever and the world to finally become what everyone had hoped and yearned for, pure music and vegetation?

Then I thought about the companions from my youth and myself. We, who had raised our voices half a lifetime ago, intending to sing summer over the land forever. Then we firmly believed that it was possible. But autumn has arrived again, and some of them have flown while others are silent and prepare to leave. A few still peep from time to time and lift their wings like the emigrant who has boarded a ship and waves his hand in parting.

The greatest fear of all is to be the last plover.

Translated by Árný Hjaltadóttir

7. The Death of Old Guðmundur the Student: Half-stolen and Half-created

NEW YEAR'S EVE was a delightful winter evening. The weather was as pleasant as a mild spring, but the atmosphere lighter and cleaner. The breeze from the glacier played around one with vitalizing warmth, and one even had the feeling that the snow itself would be warm and soft like a soft, clean, downy quilt. The light from the moon and the stars was milder than any sunshine, and not as bright. The half-thawed pasture opened before one's eyes, covered with snow in some spots and clear of it in others, as if the Christmas thaw had made it into a trusty covenant between summer-suntan and winter severity.

New Year's Eve was bright and mild. If one had to choose between this evening and the most beautiful summer day one could remember, and one could only have one of them, one would have to draw straws for them. No human mind, having a keen sense for weather changes, could decide between them any other way.

Reverend Hákon also felt it in his bones. He was in good spirits and light-of-foot, though he was by now sixty-five. The distance between the farms, Garður and Gerði, was very short, and he didn't mind it, even though night had fallen and he was alone. He didn't have to preach in the church at Garður in the morning. Sveinbjörn, his assistant, was to do that. Consequently, he was relieved, exhausted and depleted as he was from forty years of preaching, all about the same subject matter. Even a man of average intelligence will agree that it must be tiresome to recite the same verse for a whole lifetime, even though it be the most beautiful of all verses, if nothing could be changed but the voice.

Reverend Hákon's mind was engrossed with memories and hopes this New Year's Eve. Old Reverend Guðmundur the Student had sent for him from Gerði and asked him to come to see him this night. Guðmundur had been bedridden for some time and was considered to be on his deathbed. They had been together many a night in the past. They were the same age, schoolmates, and almost intimate friends. Apart from that, they had nothing in common. Providence had given Hákon this fortunate, average intelligence, which made him a respectable, noble country man, and now finally a noble pastor. Guðmundur's life had been rather dissipated. No one challenged his intelligence, though it was disputed what kind of man he was. Few remembered him for kindness; most were afraid of his behaviour and his intelligence. They could not comprehend that any but mischief-makers needed such a great intelligence. The public suspected him of being a misfit, though no one could point to anything he had done that was especially bad.

Reverend Hákon's memories centred on thoughts about how sad it was, how little Guðmundur's great abilities had benefited him. And then Guðmundur's life story came to mind, from the time he was a reckless and noble-minded youth who loved his mother enormously. They had been brought up in the same neighbourhood.

The school years approached. In the beginning, Guðmundur was without envy the most popular amongst all his classmates. It was as if they subconsciously trusted him to do almost anything, as if nothing were too hard for him and he were destined to be a great man. In the final years Guðmundur's popularity subsided somewhat. He seemed to have become alienated from the school life, was no longer a child-adult like the others, who learn what is put before them. Intelligence, which doubts received knowledge, is always self-willed and conceited in the eyes of the excessively educated simpleton. He got into disputes and quarrels and became more and more isolated. Although it appeared to be an easy task to conquer this insignificant hero through the approved, combined and immoveable wisdom of numerous sages and teachers, upon which the educational system was based, Guðmundur was sometimes extremely intense in his thoughts and difficult to refute while defending his cause. Moreover, his answers were so reasonably sound that, when his opponents knew he must have lost, they felt that their own victory was not as reassuring as it ought to be, and so they became quite annoyed with him. Nevertheless, Guðmundur graduated and could have become a pastor, but he completely refused to do so, even though his fiancée broke off their betrothal because her parents did not feel that she would be well-provided-for unless she became the wife of a pastor.

Reverend Hákon still remembered how he had urged Guðmundur to change his plans and how Guðmundur had abolished the idea, claiming that to him the ordination oath was disgusting. No matter how Hákon tried to convince him that one's promise to work at the highest and the most elevated calling in the world could never be questioned, even though one's strength might not endure, Guðmundur just smiled and turned a deaf ear to his good advice, maintaining that what was right for Hákon wasn't equally so for all men.

Hákon still clearly remembered Guðmundur's answer when he finally asked him in earnest if he had picked up the books of Arius or Zwingli. In those days, Hákon wasn't aware of any other such dreadful heretics, and then only from quotes from and confutations about them – long since dead and gone. It never crossed his mind that Guðmundur could have become a Catholic; he was a Prostestant soul by blood and upbringing for whom that ungodly church couldn't have offered any money. Guðmundur laid his hand on Hákon's shoulder.

"Listen, friend," he said, "do you remember Skúli, the quack doctor, who never knew what ailed any patient and always said that it was probably a bug of some kind – or old Finnur at Fjárvanki, who always answered, if he lost an animal and was asked what had caused it, 'Oh, it surely must have eaten grass and been poisoned by it!' Your conception is the same. I don't know if I remember what Arius and Zwingli are supposed to have said, except if I look it up. Those are things that have confused me, if you wish to put it that way. Do you remember when I blurted out that the Edda and the Bible were inspired by the same concepts, when a few of us boys sat together last year and the conversation turned to mythology? What a debate we had, and what stories! At first I unintentionally let it out without even having thought about it. I was certain that I was wrong and thought that I would be defeated at the first protest. Then I started defending it, and I was shocked at all that I found and argued for. It was like unexpectedly seeing through hills and woods. In my mind a new world of contexts and arguments opened up, whose existence I hadn't known of earlier. Now it covers all the religions that I know of, and even the creation itself is turned on its head, so that in the beginning man created God. That's how religious doctrines ran aground. Then there's doctrine and conduct; until then I would have fully maintained that they were one and the same and blamed any difference on the shortcomings of the believers, as others have done. Doctrine is believed everywhere; that's not lacking. Then there was Judas; conduct sells doctrine for a price, like he did. I noticed this recently and lost the respect I had for it. Then there are a few men like you, for instance, who are honest and good; therefore I like you and can't engage in quarrels with you, or you with me. Their moral consciousness rests upon all that's good and beautiful in the doctrine. It isn't strong enough to stand alone but coils itself around the beautiful commandments and promises, because they are by nature true to themselves though they may be nothing but imagination. But there's a remedy for all reason; it is called hunger. When I've consumed enough of that, I'll apply for a pastorate."

Hákon recalled how shocked he was at Guðmundur and himself: Guðmundur's preposterous ideas were almost atheistic, and he himself was hesitant to rebuke and correct them. But the only comment he could think of was, "What are you going to do?"

"I can't serve the church at present," said Guðmundur. "By its nature it can't be morally pure. The pastor can't address Björn, the lawbreaker, from the pulpit with these words: 'Björn, you're a criminal.' I believe that would be called slander. He can say only that 'the world is in the hands of the wicked,' so that Björn won't assume this refers to him particularly, though this is exactly what he ought to do. But because I'm a scholar, educated for a position, and useless for physical work, except perhaps for fighting, I must get some kind of paid employment. It's true that justice is blind, but it can make a judgement based on its opinion and say to the thief, 'You are a thief!' at the very least. I think I'll try my hand at being an executioner."

But Guðmundur never became an executioner. After ten difficult vagabond years many people became familiar with Guðmundur the Student. When he had become a pastor, Reverend Guðmundur the Student was well-known in his district, although men could hardly explain why; he had left behind nothing better or worse than any other pastor, at least nothing that men could clearly point to.

In those days, it was Reverend Hákon who disapproved of him the most; yet he had also felt a warm affection for him. Guðmundur's intellectual delusions had not been mended. "Why did you take a pastorate?" Reverend Hákon asked him, as if he had never encouraged him to do so. "To pay the devil with his own currency," answered Guðmundur, "or whatever it is that restricted my job opportunity, took my future wife from me, and shredded me into a seaman's sweater."

Reverend Guðmundur the Student became a curiously disagreeable splinter in the flesh of his own class. It was hardly possible to criticize his discharge of office; he did everything legally. But his conversations and stories about himself, even in public, went too far for clerical modesty. And there was hardly any breach of conduct concerning the Ten Commandments, with the exception of the fifth, which he didn't indicate was a daily coincidence with him. And he always found an identical example among other holy men, forefathers, apostles, church fathers, even in Christ Himself, for speaking disrespectfully of learned men and spiritual leaders. But as each man is fettered by his own folly, so each of his colleagues had their shortcomings and knew that the stories were really about themselves and that there was more than one about some of them. Yet they couldn't acknowledge it and tried either to make some excuse for all his weaknesses or pretended it was all a joke. The worst of it was that most of his stories about his crimes, according to the holy men, resembled the very things which men blamed the archdeacon for doing.

In Hákon's company Guðmundur laughed at all of it. "I've often challenged them openly to cast the first stone," he said, "but none of them dares. They are afraid they might hit themselves." Reverend Guðmundur was unpopular, except among a few individuals who kept a low profile and whom no one respected. Finally, the archdeacon engaged in a long and complicated lawsuit against a poor, insignificant farmer concerning additional buildings. No one knew where the farmer had received his ardour and jurisprudence from, but many suspected that Guðmundur was his trusted adviser. And whatever course the case took, all those with less knowledge distrusted Guðmundur.

After a few years, Guðmundur said to his friend Hákon, "Now I've resigned my pastorship." "What a great troublemaker you are, Mundi," answered Reverend Hákon. "With your intelligence and with a bit more caution you could have become archdeacon before Reverend Jón." "Do you remember how the trees chose their king, Hákon my friend," said Guðmundur, and grinned. "The fig tree flatly refused the title and the pine tree abdicated, but the thorn bush was greedy for a kingdom and needed no coaxing. The one who is himself free has aversion to governing others. We were not made to govern."

Reverend Guðmundur vacated his office easily. Yet he was most disturbed when it was rumoured that his resignation had come about through the archdeacon's doings and quite against his own wishes. The people in the district feared their gentlemanly, law-scheming, deceitful archdeacon even more than before, even though he lost the suit concerning the poor farmer's additional buildings.

Then Reverend Guðmundur the Student moved to Gerði, which was the closest farm to Garður. There he lived as a common farmer. Sometimes he went to church, but he never received communion. The parishioners took no offence; they knew that Guðmundur was as well-educated as Reverend Hákon, and it didn't surprise them that two coopers weren't buying casks from each other. Reverend Hákon knew what the problem was, but he ignored it, even though it grieved him. He had the foreboding that it wasn't a dogma learned by rote, nor a well-contemplated view of life, that was creating this chaos, but rather it was a deep-rooted quality, the whole psychology of that soul he himself was deeply fond of.

Reverend Guðmundur neither fell nor rose in rank in the eyes of the upper class after he left his office. They condoned him like a sheep from a poorer sheep-pen, which upbringing and custom had without reason put into their manger and therefore must be tolerated. He was esteemed especially by the sea rakes and the homeless, and a few unfortunate men were as deeply fond of him as Reverend Hákon was. He could almost have gathered around himself the tramps and the trouble-makers and would have cultivated them, if he had been able to multiply his fish and bread by a miracle.

But wasn't it likely that Guðmundur's religious beliefs would change for the better, at the eleventh hour, when he was probably on his deathbed? Hopefully. That was undoubtedly the message.

Reverend Hákon's thoughts were somewhat along this line on his way from Garður down to Gerði. His thoughts had only hinted at this meaning in some places and wove themselves into each other. He reached the entrance to the house at Gerði.

In the narrow side apartment in the north end of the living room at Gerði lay an old man in the alcove within. It was old Guðmundur the Student. Reverend Hákon sat down by his bedside. The head on the pillow showed little sign of fear with its long, thin hair, which fell in equally long strands down each cheek and in a smooth silver-grey silk trail around the large forehead, almost like a flexible square on this handsome head with the prominently-featured face and long cheeks, which old age and the deathbed had changed so little, except for hue and complexion. It had been so harshly carved, only bare skin over the strong bones. The nose was high and curved. The eyes should be called dark for want of better words to describe the colour of the matted-blue of the ice and the sunspots on a mountain side, this diffusion of light yellow and iron grey, which a man's eye can occasionally acquire. His eyebrows were thick and bushy; the wrinkles in his brows showed that they had often either been relaxed or furrowed in deep thought. Now they were motionless beneath the weight of sickness. Nothing else stood out from beneath the covers but his head and right hand, which wrapped itself, large and knotted, around the hand of Reverend Hákon. Yet it was apparent, even through the bedclothes, that the man was large, like men become aware of the size of a fallen tree in a forest, even though it has shrivelled up on the inside and almost sunk into the earth.

"I sent for you, old friend," said Guðmundur, "to be with me on the last New Year's Eve we've left together, and to make you my executor for the new year over my few possessions, which we're going to distribute. I won't last long enough to do it myself. I've always been able to sleep most soundly in the morning."

Revered Hákon was somewhat startled by this prophecy, but could say nothing more than that God could do what seemed hopeless to men, and that he himself had expected Guðmundur's condition to be much worse, but that now he thought it likely that he would last longer still.

Guðmundur pressed Reverend Hákon's hand as firmly and affectionately as his strength allowed. "Let's not attempt to make misleading statements about death, my friend!" he said. "If the tree in the woods could speak, it could often say with certainty that one more stroke could make it fall when it feels itself tremble on its foundation. Twice the sickness became so bad that I barely survived it. Tonight it'll happen again for the third and last time. Then it's finished. We've had many enjoyable New Year's eves together, and it's good to end things in this way. There on the table are our old bottle and my silver glass and my pipe. Celebrate with me New Year's Eve like we've done since we were wee lads and tried a duet in my mother's room. It isn't because I'm in low spirits, that I can't join in with you now."

Reverend Hákon did not feel like celebrating, but he could not refuse Guðmundur's request. So he lit the pipe and calmed down, perhaps because he was doing something.

"Now I'm pleased with you," said Guðmundur, and smiled his old smile. "That's how it should be. It reminds me of the times in my life when you were the only man who didn't think I was a lost sheep. Since Mother died you were sometimes the only one who trusted the boy in me, so that I never quite failed him altogether, even when I was dealing with such wretched men like Reverend Jón, the archdeacon;

with my eye-for-an-eye attitude I felt I couldn't be cruel enough to him."

"No, no," said Reverend Hákon, "now you're talking nonsense. On your deathbed you don't hate anyone. You must forgive – forgive everything."

"Forgive!" repeated Guðmundur. "Do you know what you are asking, Hákon? To forgive, to excuse wickedness! Refute what was the noblest in my nature, to say that I agree with villainy! No, no! Archdeacon Reverend Jón could be the highest ranking archangel on the other side for all I care; I wouldn't prevent it, even if I could, for the minor problem he caused me. It was welcomed. But he was a bully to the end of his life. If I say otherwise, then I would be compromising with baseness, and that I won't do on my deathbed, even if all the people in the world begged me to and forgave me for doing so. And even if they would be saved by it, I would rather go to hell with the truth, consoling myself with the fact that we were at least the honest minority. But it probably won't come to that. Reverend Jón has by now probably become an angel. He needed to, and hopefully I'll get some rest."

"Not so!" answered Reverend Hákon. "You yourself will be brought to the land where all human misunderstandings disappear, where agony and regret don't exist."

"And what would I do there, where all are happy, with no one to side with, with no one to lend a hand to, and no prejudice to deal with? Old Guðmundur the Student would soon be bored with such slumber. He would compose a humorous verse about it, right in the middle of 'Te deum.' Old Guðmundur the Student who chose to lose his future wife rather than be ordained pastor when it pricked his conscience, would be badly seated in the lap of Abraham, who wanted to sacrifice his son, even though he considered it wrong. Such misunderstandings can never be brought to account. Old Guðmundur the Student would get into disputes there with Jacob, Isaac's son, as he did with the late archdeacon, over how Jacob long ago gained profits from his starving brother with his leftover pea soup. But then there isn't much point in that. I'm exhausted and tired of the struggle, and what awaits me is nothing but rest."

"Far from it, far from it," said Reverend Hákon, who in his

confusion couldn't give answers in such difficult situations, and didn't want to believe them either. "You aren't serious about those radical thoughts."

"I've never joked with you about such things, and least of all now," said Guðmundur. "Your belief is your nature, to see the good in all. You are sincere, but you don't have the eye of the reformer, who sees injustice as clearly as, or better than, reconciliation and compromise. My opinions aren't radical either. I don't expect any wickedness. I couldn't go wrong. I wouldn't be without comfort down there in the flames, I who know no greater happiness than to do my best, because it makes one mature and more content. I'd try to rake a few sparks away from some wretched fellow who could stand the heat less than I. Nor would I be shocked by those who would be tormented by pangs of conscience, though that might be a bit fanatical. I'd know by the poor wretches' admittance that they hadn't reformed as they should have done, and their regret over wicked amusements, which they have to overcome, would be the first sign of recovery and self-improvement, although it seems to be rather impudent, since they are eternal and can't do away with themselves as they can in this life. As you can see, I'm not suitable for either of the places that religion intends for men. I'm not qualified for them, and I'm not able to execute my intentions. Rest is what is intended for me, and I wish for nothing else."

"But you wish for that which will soon be granted, to see your mother again, where you'll both feel well," answered Reverend Hákon, quite certain that he touched the most sensitive cord.

"On the contrary," said Guðmundur, "I wish least of all to see her, because I've loved her the most of all people, my mother, who loved her boy and trusted him to become that man whom she thought to be the best. No, that would be too much of a disappointment, to see her boy having become the old Guðmundur. She wouldn't recognize him. And yet, her boy had to become exactly this old man, if he weren't to betray himself and her. No, I wouldn't want to annoy her. I couldn't do it. Then she wouldn't be as completely happy as we believe she is. And don't say that our personalities, Mother's and mine, could change in such a way at the hour of death that this wouldn't matter. Because then it wouldn't be her or me any longer, who knew each other and loved one another, because we were the ones we were, otherwise we'd have been different people. Old Guðmundur the Student deserves his rest."

Hákon became silent. He smoked faster and stopped thinking as one who sees his trusted child ignore his warning and take the road that to him is impassable, without being able to do anything but hope for the best and avoid thinking about what he once thought he knew.

After a short silence, Guðmundur said, "We must put this out of our minds, my friend. I'm leaving, and I must give you the message. Don't let Reverend Sveinbjörn hold a sermon over me when I'm dead. Do it yourself, and say what you want about me. It won't be anything less than what you think I deserve. I don't like Reverend Sveinbjörn's fashionable liberalism. This vagueness, which wants to ingratiate itself with every old superstition and court all new protests, and mix them all up, is in the direction of old Abraham. He wants to sacrifice Isaac, although reason and affection incessantly repeat that it is a crime, only because someone whom you fear or revere tells you to do so. This mixture of superstition and reason is perhaps a natural momentary balance of the old, which has lost its power, and of the new, which is as yet undeveloped, but I have an aversion to it. It is a cancerous sore on the sincerity of the nation. I gave him my resignation in this life, and he has no right to speak over my earthly remains. There are $200 in the drawer of my table. Get Þorvaldur in Fótaskinna to dig my grave and to put me into it. Give him fifty dollars for it. He lives without any means of support, and before the winter is over he will steal from someone to support himself and his own. His personality is such that to steal would not bother him as much as it would to take charity. He'll be caught and therefore be in trouble for the rest of his life. Perhaps these fifty dollars will support him this time around. Give the same job to Kolbeinn in Kaldrandi and pay him the same. He put his energy and resources into some improvements on his small farm and worked up a higher land-rent, and his household will probably break up because of it. Then there's old Einar the Singer. Providence forgot to give him foresight and energy, but endowed him with the most beautiful voice and then set him down on land where not even one mouthful can be gained for a beautiful voice, except maybe for a meal thrown one's way at the common table at a few banquets. And finally, there is old Bergur in Selhagi. He doesn't have a dollar to his name and plans to sell his only cow, so that he may be able to send little Gestur south to a relative of his, who offered to send him to school. To that stripling the ardent desire for knowledge will be an ill-fated gift, like Niels's and Daði's, if nothing is done about it. The school will destroy his chance of becoming a man, but his stomach will be left intact and it will give it bread. You pay Einar and Bergur fifty dollars each for the same job that is intended for the others. Other belongings I have already disposed of. Good night, Hákon my comrade, and thank you for your companionship. Now the alleviation of my pain is almost over. I know what's coming. One more request. It's thought that one lives one's youth over in one's last moments. I felt something like it before when I had the fits, when I came closest to the end, but my mind couldn't remember quite how it was when I became conscious again. What's wrong with the idea that consciousness is a circle that closes where it begins? Sit down at the table and sing with me 'Rise up my soul anew,' as you remember my mother used to sing it for us New Year's Morning, when we were little boys. And so farewell."

Revered Hákon did as he was asked. He sang verse after verse in a weak, tearful voice. The daylight shone through the window. He thought he heard a long, drawn breath behind him. Old Guðmundur the Student lay there motionless and tranquil as if he were asleep. His head had sunk down onto his chest and his heart didn't stir. He was lifeless.

Hákon laid Guðmundur's hands upon his chest and closed his eyelids. He didn't doubt that Guðmundur had told the truth and knew what to expect. He stroked his cheek, which was starting to feel cool to the touch, as men do when they say goodbye to a sleeping child.

"No, no, whatever is said, I wouldn't be happy in heaven either, if you couldn't be there."

Outside New Year's Day was dawning. Inside the glimmer of a new belief began.

Translated by Árný Hjaltadóttir

8. The New Hat

IT WAS ADVENT, and never had there been so few visitors to
Newdale nor so little happening since the settlement began in the
spring. Less than half the valley was settled, and the farms were far
apart. When the neighbours on rare occasions met, they sat yawning
half the time they could spare for each other. The story about when
Hatta calved and how it happened, and guesses about when Sigvaldi's
Tobba would get pregnant, had to come to an end at some point, like
all earthly and transitory things. The farmers had lost all hope that
more people would move to the valley that year; they pottered about
silently, still nourishing the hope of living in a bigger settlement,
though in one where nobody would take land next to them.

Premonitions and miracles had actually taken place far away out
in the wide world, and the people of the valley could have discussed
them in the common, shortsighted and subjective fashion, because
they were well-educated and not a savage people, and they always
read a few newspapers, but much of their content was not even of
interest to any of them and therefore forgotten as soon as it was read.
The discussions centred on general news, especially if they found it
exciting, such as if some gangster was said to have committed an old-
fashioned crime in a more unusual way than they had ever heard of.
They skipped the news of the peace conference in the Hague; it did
not concern either the well-being or welfare of the people of the
valley. Even there in the valley, in this little, newly cultivated place
at the edge of human colonization, there were indications of the
individual's humane practicality, which fate had placed in the seat of
a despot and was bound to go on a penitential pilgrimage from the
political freedom of the inherited ignorance of the democracies
themselves. No one is liberal unless he himself has felt the chains.
Kipling's jingoistic songs are recited from the minds of proud
Englishmen, but Tolstoy's humane exhortations come from the heart
of the Siberian exile. Generation after generation and century after
century, the ancestors of these men of the valley had lived isolated and
far away from such extremes in human society. They were as
indifferent to the world's major events as they were to the question of
how Reverend Oddur's oil bag and Reverend Jens's steamship had

been able to grow into the teachings of Christ, as their church journal had once indicated. The people of Newdale were only a little splash of an Icelandic low tide that called itself "western immigration," and it had solidified there in the flat-bottomed hollow on the prairie that they called Newdale.

When the lack of news was at its worst in Newdale, help was close at hand, as it always is except at the hour of death. One of the men of the valley came home from the city, which in itself was a noteworthy event, though even more amazing was the fact that he was wearing a new hat. Not that a hat had never been seen in the settlement, because the people of Newdale were educated and hats were part of their everyday outfit, but they were mostly old, cheap hats, and this hat was new and smart and appeared to be a fine specimen. No one could imagine what kind of exorbitant price had been paid for such a treasure, and although almost every man and woman in the settlement did his or her best to come up with a price, it was nonetheless like a common misfortune in the minds of the people that these conjectures were all no more than unreliable guesses, which could all be more or less inaccurate. Even though this was a great catastrophe, which could not be avoided because the owner of the hat refused to say anything specific no matter how the topic was broached, it was a consolation that the discussion was based on the one thing that was indisputable, and that was that the owner of the hat was as poor as everyone else in Newdale in those days. It was clear that a consider-able addition to the winter stock, of which there was a shortage everywhere, could have been got for the price of the hat, if thrifty men, as they all were, had had a say in the matter.

In this way the story of the hat lasted day after day almost until winter solstice. In the end it was, however, discussed parallel with another matter, which also became significant. It was less than two weeks until St. Þorlákur's Day, and it was uncertain if anyone in the settlement, and in that case who, would have a slice of meat left for Christmas.

The hat was hardly mentioned after the New Year. Everyone had become tired of discussing it. Most of them had seen it and now found that there was nothing remarkable about it. No one commented on it when it disappeared, even though it was short-lived. It blew off the owner's head in a storm on Ash Wednesday and became both shabby and dented. The owner did not live long either. Two years after the story of the hat began, one of the people of Newdale wrote a long article in one of the Icelandic newspapers called *News from the Newdale Settlement*. Only the last five lines contained any news, but the introduction was, on the other hand, very detailed. It repeatedly stated that because none of the many people of Newdale, who were intelligent and good writers, had yet taken it upon himself to inform the world about the events that had taken place there, and that were no less interesting than news from other settlements, the author of the article now took the first step, but only half-heartedly; he was so afraid that such a difficult task might be beyond his capacity. It was only because more competent men shirked the issue that he who was least competent stepped forward. At the end of this poignantly humble monologue he added that recently a man in the settlement had been injured in a threshing-machine accident and had died. The man referred to was the owner of the hat. This reveals man's superiority over dead things; few think about a blown-away hat, except the owner, but the death of a man may get into the newspapers.

In the second issue of *News from the Newdale Settlement*, which came out twelve months later and was written by the same man, it was mentioned that the widow of the man, "the one who was injured in a threshing-machine accident and had died," had been married by "the priest, Reverend Baggi," a while ago. It must certainly have been a consolation to those who were concerned that the widow was alone and felt sorry for her.

Nowadays everyday events like a hat blowing away are hardly interesting. If, for example, Ezekiel in days of yore had told about the blown-away hat as a prophetic vision, and if Paul of Tarsus a few centuries later had referred to the owner's tragic end in an epistle, our eyes would have been opened, and we would have seemed to see an obscure connection between these events and been certain that at one time Providence had begun a conversation with our ancestors in a symbolic language. But even though we have lost the apostolic ability to see omens of future events in the legends of antiquity, we are now more able to analyse the consequences of what takes place in the world. And no one can as yet see the end results of the hat's appearance in Newdale. Twenty years have now passed since it was first seen there, but each year its influences become steadily more impressive and clear.

You give a wry smile, reader, and I know what you are smiling at. You read what others have written for their own admonition and notice that you've caught me in a major chronological error. The peace conference was last year; the hat entered the story the same autumn, but nonetheless twenty years have passed in Newdale. What fiction! You can make of it as much as you like, dear reader, but spare me one thing: do not call it anachronism or some such fancy word that common people do not understand and are scared of, because that would finish me off among the people. Of course it is childish of us common people to be so afraid of learning that it need only be formal-sounding to scare us, even though we do not understand the words. But nothing can be done about that; it is a heritage we cannot shake off. We got it from our pious fathers, who listened with respect to their priest exorcising the evil spirits out of the babies he had to baptize in many attacks of broken Latin. Now if you forgive me this detail, my kind and truthful reader, I shall make a small concession to you in return. Do not read further than this chronological error until twenty years from now, and I shall bet you a new, silk hat, against the hat that blew away, that the spirit of the age in Newdale fits the year just like it did yesterday. I am serious about this, and I do not intend to lose a silk hat, either dead or alive.

Torfi and Teitur were neighbours living opposite each other in the middle of Newdale, promising farmers and friends, before the news of the hat came out. Because of their position in the settlement and their boldness in general discussions about local matters, they could not avoid putting in a word regarding the folk tale about the hat. In the beginning, they did not agree, and followed each their own theory. Torfi followed the one that was most common, that the hat had been bought at an expensive price and been an unwise purchase, and proved it with the story about old Franklin and his flute. Teitur said that the hat had been given to the man by an acquaintance of his in the city and had in reality been discarded by some gentleman, who thought it did not suit him, and rarely used it. Teitur claimed that he had this information from the owner himself. On the basis of this slight difference of opinion, Teitur and Torfi once began a debate, first on the basis of probabilities, which were soon exhausted, next with jokes, which did not get them far either, and finally with sarcastic remarks, which proved the most effective. Although neither of them had become very angry, both were afterwards annoyed with themselves, because both were convinced that their argument was the better and even considered it likely that there was something that remained unpaid. They met and talked as cheerfully as before, and without a grudge, but from then on they competed in everything. If Teitur went right, Torfi went left, or the other way around. They did not do this deliberately, for the paths to chieftaincy in Newdale were not wide enough for more than one crown for each position, which was too small for two heads or more.

Teitur had a nice house; his farm consisted of many impressive buildings and more than he could afford. Therefore he was in debt. More than his annual profit went into paying interest. In lean years the debts were heavier than those that the Jews in ancient times paid their priests and Jehovah, ten percent of all products, but in bad years all profits were used exclusively for the needs of the home. Teitur was always in financial difficulties, but he found it worth the trouble when he looked at his new house and compared it with Torfi's old shack on the other side of the valley.

Torfi was not particularly interested in large-scale buildings. He was more interested in vast fields and big landownership. Wherever a strip of land was for sale at a bargain price, he got his hands on it, not least in Teitur's neighbourhood. Even though he sometimes found that the work involved in taking care of all this land was almost killing him, he always calmed down when he thought about the fact that Teitur's house would fall apart and go down in value each year, whereas his own land gave profit and constantly increased in value. Nonetheless, the old shack often bothered him. His wife often and firmly said, especially when guests were listening, that it was due to his miserliness and tastelessness that she did not have as nice a house as Teitur's wife had.

Both housewives certainly have had many pleasures from a nice home and a fine harvest. They probably never suspected to what a great extent that was owing to the new hat.

The same was the case in politics. Torfi and Teitur never belonged to the same party. If Torfi was Conservative, Teitur was Progressive, or the other way around. Torfi was a pillar of the congregation and supported the church's concerns, which are similar to those of usurer societies – not to insult the government of the day, whatever it is called, if it has left all their perks alone. Institutions protected by law do not throw themselves into prospective agreements with a future power, unless reactionaries form an alliance with them. Torfi, however, realized that he followed the Conservative Party against his convictions in matters of tax protectionist tariffs. He was a tight-fisted farmer and realized that it cost him money to pay rich people interest, but still he maintained and defended this policy with the arrogance of a deliberately weak argument.

Teitur supported the Liberal Party and the lowering of tariffs, but was nonetheless no more pleased with himself than Torfi was. He had become more far-sighted and realized that promises did not materialize, as those who were more familiar with these matters knew. The conventional government had woven expenditures into the system for many years to come, and the Reform Government, which took over, had to prepare sufficiently profitable income controls so that the government did not fall apart. Nothing else was possible, no matter what was promised. He had a great economist's loathing for this governmental wisdom, which, when things were so badly needed, would not sufficiently take all the money at once, like the wool off the sheep in the spring. One had to start cutting slowly from above – people went even crazier than the sheep when they lost that whole tuft of wool in one moment – and, for that, commercial tariffs were indispensably practical.

When the Conservative Party lost, Torfi nonetheless felt more at ease because of his contribution to it; he had nothing to regret, especially because Teitur had been so strongly opposed to it. Teitur was also pleased with events and found enough of an excuse in his strengthening the victory of the Liberal Party, no matter how opposed to it Torfi was.

The same happened in the next election. But then Torfi had become Liberal, because that government was in power. He had donated a bell to the church; it rang for him. Teitur had become

Conservative. He did not think that the conditions in the country had changed favourably with the change of people in Parliament, except that the weather was good and that there was a failure of the crops abroad, for which he thanked a power different from that decided in general elections. It did not matter on which side of the political fence one lived; the nation was the same, the countryside similar – only the colours of the flags were different. So Torfi had become Liberal. But neither was completely happy with his position. The hat had certainly made them pull themselves together spiritually, as a clever canvasser could make them do in his district, but they still had not reached the political maturity that makes one a slave to the opinions of one's party, which divides the political world so easily into the just (oneself and one's party) and the unjust (the gangsters and the wicked people, who do not vote for one's party). They still had not been able to completely abandon independent thinking and forming their own opinions, even though they did it silently. Even though this serves as an indisputable proof of a bit of reason in most matters, it does not suit party politics. Torfi knew from his own experience that the Liberal Party had not kept its promise to ease the burden of taxes, which he saw had become an advantage to him; it was, therefore, not correct to follow that party now, any more than when Teitur supported it. Teitur did not feel comfortable in his Conservative Party either. Even though it made little difference, it still felt a bit more disgusting to work on the side of those who made efforts to go against what one considered better, rather than to follow those on the other side who agreed with one's opinion and pretended to materialize it, although one knew that it was an empty promise.

It is still not impossible to figure out what reforms can be traced back to the appearance of the hat in Newdale.

Torfi supported the Church and administered the congregation. Teitur did not belong to the Church and was a Unitarian. Torfi was greatly involved in the building of a church, in setting up regulations for the congregation, and in the election of a priest, and he was indefatigable in raising money for these matters. But here his religious life ended. He provided what he could afford to what he called Christianity: money and leadership. His inner religious life was non-existent. When he looked across the slope to his neighbour, Teitur, a

Unitarian, he could not help thinking that it was a blemish on the community on the other side not to have a church. Then he always decided to make the next "sacrifice" a bit bigger than he had originally planned, so that his church could buy a fine bell or a beautiful pulpit. Even though he did not fully believe the doctrine about eternal hellfire (because he was an Icelander and a truly good man) and defended it with all his might only when it was attacked (like priests do these days), and he found that he had to protest violently to do it, he could not tear the idea out of his heart, when he looked homewards to the disbeliever opposite his farm, that the Scripture speaks of "indistinguishable fire" and "immortal serpents." At least there must be a big difference. What would be the use of having spent many hundreds of dollars on the Otherlife and never having forsaken one's faith if everyone got the same treatment in the end?

The hat had, of course, never shown signs and worked miracles like St. Anne's shrine had. But it had strengthened the Church in Newdale considerably, even though few people knew – an everyday hat, as it had been, that had perished among a religious group of people who do not care about relics.

Teitur was not really a Unitarian either. He had to take on this name to differentiate himself from Torfi, who called himself a Christian in every second word after he got involved in the building of the church. Teitur had many spiritual followers, both inside and outside the congregation, who believed that Teitur would go the most direct and most pleasant way to eternal life in the end, even though they declined to call themselves Unitarians.

Incredible as it may seem, the hat, and not the priest, blazed a new trail for theology in Newdale.

Strangers might think that the journalist I mentioned above, and not Teitur, had become a spiritual leader in Newdale after Torfi and the priest. The beginning of his article showed that he was a likely candidate for the chieftaincy. Common people have respect for the great learning required to write an article in a newspaper, and they like humility, because they consider themselves more incompetent than others in educational matters; humility shows that learning can be general and without arrogance. But then something else came up; the journalist had not abstained from involving himself in the hat case when it was at its hottest, but he had nonetheless not supported either party. When he was east in the valley in Torfi's neighbourhood, his views on the hat were similar to the views prevailing there. When he came west to where Teitur lived, his views changed in the direction of those held there. Such a cosmopolitan feature was regarded as suspect in a remote settlement like Newdale. Moreover, in some of his articles, the journalist had not been accurate in his description of the weather and the harvest in the settlement; he had, for example, written that the average harvest on the fields was fifteen bushels, when the settlers calculated the average to be sixteen and five-eights and nowhere fifteen except on his "plot." As one might expect, they all disliked him and thought that he publicly caused the settlement shame. Even though the people of Newdale believed that learning and not punctuality formed the basis for general articles, they were hurt, and distrusted the journalist in most things.

In a peculiar way the hat had made people poor and rich in Newdale, and it had degraded them and raised them.

To be sure, Teitur totally refused to believe in eternal damnation, even though he did not completely reject the fact that training was required for each soul in the spiritual world on the other side. But often when he walked past a piece of land next to his lands and which Torfi had taken with a legal distraint from some poor man, Teitur could not help it sometimes crossing his mind that Torfi's penance in his other life might be rather long.

The influence of the hat on the spiritual life of the people in the valley is constantly spreading, and who knows when it will stop. It is true that Newdale is now considered among the most prosperous Western Icelandic settlements and among those that are praised the most for their spiritual lives. In the hands of Providence the hat has now stirred the souls in Newdale to such an extent that when politics and piety can turn into livelihoods for some of the more important men, as it will soon do there as well as elsewhere in this progressive country, then the people of Newdale can safely boast about their interests and ideas, as more important settlements are now taking the opportunity of doing.

Translated by Kirsten Wolf

9. The Seventh Day

IN SIX DAYS God created Heaven and Earth. He invented something new each day. On the seventh day He rested. Or, rather – He created the echo: the priests and the editors.

Translated by Kirsten Wolf

✳

IN DAYS OF YORE

Þorsteinn Þ. Þorsteinsson

Þorsteinn Þ. Þorsteinsson (1879-1955) was born in Svarfaðardalur. He went to the Agricultural School at Hólar in Hjaltadalur (1898-1900) and emigrated to Canada in 1901, where he settled in Winnipeg as a tradesman (painter).

Þorsteinn Þ. Þorsteinsson's publications include two volumes of poetry, *Þættir* (Winnipeg, 1918) and *Heimhugi* (Reykjavík, 1921), the anecdotes *Kossar* (Reykjavík, 1934), and the historical works *Vestmenn: Útvarpserindi um landnám Íslendinga í Vesturheimi* (Reykjavík, 1935) and *Æfintýrið frá Íslandi til Brasilíu* (Reykjavík, 1937-1938). In addition, he wrote the first three volumes of *Saga Íslendinga í Vesturheimi* (Reykjavík and Winnipeg, 1940-1945). He was also the editor of the literary periodicals *Fíflar* 1914-1919 and *Saga* 1925-1931, which contains a fair number of his poems and most of his short stories.

"In Days of Yore" is translated from "Frá fyrri dögum" in *Saga* (1926-1927), pp. 108-133. The story was reprinted in Einar H. Kvaran and Guðm. Finnbogason, eds., *Vestan um haf* (Reykjavík, 1930), pp. 377-397.

IN THE OLD DAYS when the northwestern part of Canada was being settled, and the railway across the enormous country was under construction, it was often difficult to find work in the towns and cities. The same was the case in Winnipeg. A large number of day labourers left for the countryside in the summer season, and many found employment on the construction of the railway.

The Icelanders were then newly settled in this country, and every year a group of them emigrated west. They were very poor during those years, as is, in fact, still the case with them as it is with a great number of other nations. Most of them found it hard enough to provide for themselves: nonetheless, helpfulness seems to have been more common then than it is in Winnipeg nowadays, judging by the stories that are told. Many left the city to earn money, even though they had to say goodbye to their families to go many hundreds of miles away and leave behind their children and wives more in the care of God and good neighbours than with the knowledge that there were sufficient means for the household left behind. Of course, many things were cheap in those days, but then the currency was expensive as well and required a lot of hard work, so that each cent was often paid for with countless drops of sweat.

Gríma Árdal lived in the Icelandic part of Winnipeg. She was a widow, in poor health, and had many children. Her eldest son, Kári, was sixteen years old. He could not find employment in Winnipeg, but as he was big and clever and keen to help his poor mother, she let him have his way to go to work for the railway, where he received almost the same wages as adult workers. Kári had left early in the spring, and his mother did not expect him back until late in the autumn.

Gríma's husband, Þórður Jónsson from Árdalir, had died one year earlier, but at that time life insurance was not as common as it is now, and he hardly left Gríma anything except the children and his reputation as an honourable man.

Þórður had a brother, Þorsteinn, who had emigrated west before him. He went to the United States and had called himself – or been called – Stoney Dal. No Icelander had heard of him for more than ten years. Þorsteinn had not been fond of hard work. He had made it as far as the fourth grade of grammar school in Reykjavík, but had been forced to stop because of lack of money and disorderliness. Soon after his arrival in the United States, people said that he was hanging out with experienced gamblers and was doing nothing but playing for money, especially poker, when he was last heard of. It was not surprising, therefore, that the Icelanders considered him dead, because in those days the revolver and sheath knife were always in use if something came up. Moreover, they often played in places the police did not know of or did not care to visit, and the cities were slow to miss unknown foreigners who silently and without complaint disappeared into eternity.

Kári was working out west in the Rocky Mountains on the construction of the Canadian Pacific Railroad, which connected

Canada from coast to coast, about three thousand miles, on the seventh of November 1885, when the last iron nail was driven in by Donald Smith (Lord Strathcona) in Craigellachie to secure the last rail of this big railway.

For fourteen years, hands and heads had been united in this great enterprise. Eleven different routes had been surveyed with much patience over the Rocky Mountains in order to find the very best, although ten were measured in vain. But Canada paid the CPR manifold and thousandfold for all its toil, and the company still pays enormous taxes.

The men who got together there out west in the mountains and wastelands were not all good and morally upright. But if people today took the time to look beneath their fashionable make-up and veneer of civility, then appearances would be no better now than they were then, and the morals would probably be similar, if the care and conditions were the same.

Many workers had no home except the Wild West, which was now being tamed. They saved up their day's wages for half or a whole year. Then one day they would take off to some village that was being built, to go on a one- or two-week binge, return empty-handed and crazed, only to start working and saving up all over again for a new binge. Others never saved up anything and immediately spent the money on booze and gambling. But some saved up for old age and for the future, and did not spend more than what was absolutely necessary.

Nonetheless, the majority of those who worked on the construction and supervision of the railway were family men from here and there, who had responsibilities of one kind or another and spent nothing on unnecessary things but saved up everything in order to support their home, family and loved ones. But no one became rich or made others rich on the wages. The average salary on the construction was one or two dollars a day, but no more than one dollar and a quarter for those who inspected and repaired the work that was completed. And the four dollars per week that had to be paid for food cut into the salary, and therefore some tried to feed themselves, but that was kind of an emergency measure and most gave up on it.

Kári had saved up almost two hundred dollars. He had not spent as much as one cent unnecessarily, and, like a child, as indeed he was, he was looking forward to coming home to his mother and giving her the money, and to seeing his brothers and sisters and other acquaintances. He eagerly counted the weeks. Now only one week remained until his departure. For such a young man, he had worked like a berserk. Outdoor life and youthfulness quickly make up for exhaustion when regular and sufficient rest is taken at the end of each working day. In his mind he saw his mother dragging herself with little strength to the English women's houses to wash their clothes and floors, and clean their houses high and low, while his brothers and sisters, in second-hand clothes given to them by the English women, played around on the muddy road and yard in front of and around the small, low, wooden shack, which their dear father had thrown together during his last year.

Kári had saved $100, and the last leg of his exile was coming to an end. Each time he thought about his return he envisaged his mother hugging him, patting him and kissing him for the money he brought her, because she was to get all the money. He wasn't going to spend one cent on himself – only a little on sweets for his brothers and sisters, so that the joy would be as complete as possible. A warm wave of joy of a son's love went through his soul and gently touched his nerves and feelings each time this thought came to mind. He knew how sincerely happy his mother would be, and how tenderly she would thank him, her big and clever boy, when he came home to her from the wilderness with his hands full of money. And his brothers and sisters! They would all be fighting over the sweets, laughing and jumping all around him – the adventurer.

Such lofty intentions create an entire world of joy in the human mind long before the good deed is manifested in the world of reality. And all these beautiful and noble thoughts greatly eased each effort and exertion that this unhardened youth had to make in a merciless environment of trained workmen, who in those years had little of that sympathy for one another which the strong unions of recent years have awakened to a considerable extent and made the workers more reasonable and sociable.

In Kári's group, poker was a common pastime in the evenings after work. The main instigator was a certain supervisor. His name was Jim Dalton, and he was considered a very shrewd gambler. He went from one group to the other and often played throughout the night. And in the end he often had his hands on all the money his fellow players had available, and sometimes I.O.U.s for unreceived salaries for future workdays. The entire summer salary of many a worker had ended up in his pockets. That's how attractive a risk it was. Although the men cursed him fiercely, few resisted the temptation to try and match him.

There was an Icelander working in the same section as Kári. He was an old, good-natured fellow who took a liking to the boy. He was called Gunnlaugur Sigurðsson by Icelanders, but among English-speaking people his name was George Simpson. And since he almost always worked with Canadians, the latter name became more attached to him, and he firmly believed that it was a correct translation of his Icelandic name.

George had taught Kári to play poker when they were bored in the evenings. But instead of money they used matches, which George always had available because he smoked a lot. George never played for money, although he enjoyed the game if it was played harmlessly, as he called it. Once, when he had just arrived in the country, he had played in earnest, and his earnestness had been an expensive pleasure, because in the end he had been standing in his underwear, without money, watch, hat, shoes and pipe, and the loss of his pipe was the worst part. The only thing he had not been robbed of was the headache the next day when he got up after having played cards and drunk whisky for twenty-four hours. Then the cards had become trivial, and the bottom of the aquavit barrel was broken, so that nothing was left, not even the dregs. They did not finish everything in the barrel, however, because a few square pieces of poor-quality tobacco were left, which had been nailed to the bottom by the brewers to give their young aquavit an older taste and more distinguished flavour. But George swore that it had been a rotting polling barrel that they had been drinking from.

Kári had never gambled, but sometimes watched the players. And in order that this story is told according to the truth and nothing but the truth, as in all good Icelandic sagas, then it cannot be denied that he was tempted to try a match with them and win a few hundred dollars – at least double the amount that he intended to give Gríma, his mother. But the fear that he might lose some of his hard-earned money was stronger than the uncertain hope of profit and the longing to play. And indeed, George would not hear of such a thing, and he had considerable influence on Kári.

One evening, three days before Kári intended to return home, Jim Dalton spoke to him saying he wished to gladden him a little, this Icelandic youth from the northernmost part of the world, before he would be gone from the mountains, and gave him and a few others some drinks, though in moderation. Indeed, Kári did not want to drink much, but he did not like to refuse altogether either. Nonetheless, the alcohol had the effect that when Jim said that now he should try his luck just for fun and see if he couldn't get hold of a few extra dollars, but stop immediately, if luck turned against him, then Kári's caution yielded to the risk. George was not present and could not dissuade him. But Kári thought the risk was minimal. He could stop immediately, if he saw that he was going to lose, as Jim had said, so his mother would not suffer a great loss. And if he won! . . . Cheers to the Icelander! Then his mother would get it all.

Then they started playing. But Kári did not lose. He won – one, two, three, four, five, ten, twenty, thirty, forty, fifty dollars. He was in seventh heaven. Now he need not worry about playing. He could afford it, even if he lost. It did not occur to him to stop. And it would probably be unfair not to give his fellow players a chance. That would not be proper for an Icelander. But now he started losing, and he lost as fast as he had won. They disappeared – one, two, three, four, five, ten, twenty, thirty, forty and fifty dollars. Now he knew he had to stop. But he couldn't, and he continued to lose – five, twenty, fifty and . . . a hundred. One hundred dollars lost! He must win them back no matter what, but he didn't. He lost everything he had – all his mother's money. Nobody would lend him any, and he was in trouble. The entire spring and summer salary spent in a short time. Destitute, he, his mother, and his brothers and sisters now had to face the hard and deathly long Manitoba winter. He hardened himself so as not to let his fellow players see his feelings and the tears that welled up in his eyes, got up silently and staggered home to his bed, where he hid his face in bitter desperation and cried hopelessly for a long time. It seemed to him that he had committed such a great crime that neither his mother nor the almighty God could ever forgive him. He could not ask anybody for forgiveness for his misdeed, and unforgiven repentance leads to desperation. There was no way out. He could, of course, get home for free as a worker for the railway company, but he could not bear to come home empty-handed to his mother's poverty after all these months. And the winter was just around the corner.

Kári hardly spoke to anyone, and few minded him except George. George tried to console him, yet he cursed him for his stupidity, and Jim for his dirty trick. In fact, there were others who thought the trick Jim had played this poor youth was malicious. But Jim was their supervisor, and there was no sense of solidarity among them, so each considered it most sensible and in his own interest not to accuse anybody of anything. Many of them had experienced the same, although they were all adults, all except Kári.

The next evening an unknown traveller came to the camping site of the section in which Kári and George were located. He was a middle-aged man in appearance and carried a backpack. He was wearing workmen's clothes, blue jeans, a black shirt, and sturdy leather shoes. On his head he wore a shepherd's hat. He said that his name was Mr. Thorndale, and he asked for shelter for the night. He said that he had worked on the railway for this company for a long time many hundreds of miles west of this place and was now on his way to a small village, which he named, east of the mountains to spend the winter and rest his tired legs.

The traveller was not wearing a belt, and appeared to be carrying no weapons. When this event took place, it was not uncommon for travellers to carry knives and pistols in their belts, especially if they had money on them, although most stories of the Wild West that are told nowadays in papers and shown in films are exaggerated.

On his left side he carried a leather flask fastened to a leather strap, which was slung over his right shoulder like those who travel long distances over wasteland and desert, where there is no water. In the right pocket of his shirt a large silver cross was attached to a broad silk ribbon around his neck. It was clear that the traveller chose to have the cross rest in his pocket rather than have it hang loose on his chest. Otherwise the cross was the only peculiar thing about the man, and put him in a strange light in the minds of those who saw him.

Jim Dalton soon realized that here might be a good catch, and asked the guest if he would like to gamble since he had nothing better to do.

The guest was modest about his knowledge of gambling and said that he was used to having heavier things between his hands than scraps of paper, though to some of the workers his hands did not seem rough or weatherbeaten like the hands of those who work outdoors in Canada.

Finally, after repeated requests, he agreed to play with Jim, and they decided to meet at the gambling place half an hour later.

George had been listening to their conversation, and because he rather liked the stranger and was indignant towards the camp supervisor because of his treatment of Kári, he engaged in a conversation with him in such a way that it did not attract attention, and he advised him not to risk his money in gambling with Jim. He told him many examples in support of his point, and at last the story of Kári.

The traveller seemed indifferent to all the gambling stories, until he got to Kári. When he heard his story, he was all ears. George was not surprised. He considered the story to be worthy of attention.

"And you say the boy is very poor?" asked the traveller.

"He owns only the rags he's wearing."

"How many children does his mother in Winnipeg have?"

"Four. Kári's the fifth."

"And you said that his mother was a destitute widow?"

"Yes."

"And how long ago did this Mrs. Árdal's husband die?"

George answered as accurately as he could.

"And what are the first names of this couple? They're probably as peculiar as the Árdal name, which is very foreign."

George told him the names and that they were Icelandic.

The guest seemed to contemplate something profoundly. George thought that he was trying to think of an easy way out of playing with Jim Dalton, now that he had heard what a dangerous character he was. But the guest's words indicated that this was not the case. "It must be disagreeable to be an Icelander among the people of this country," he said. "Aren't they considered very wild and immoral?" The stranger gave George a peculiar, questioning look.

"Oh, yes. But here they don't think much about one's nationality if one's name is translated into good English so that it's easy to pronounce," said George, and there was a triumphant tone in his voice.

The guest looked sharply at him, as if he were trying to figure out what he meant. But his look immediately became milder when he realized that George's expression showed nothing but self-satisfaction, which resulted in a jovial smile on his face. "I see. So the Icelanders change their names?"

"Yes, I think so, at least some of them. I certainly wasn't christened George, and no one in my family was called Simpson before me."

"So you're Icelandic?" There was no surprise in his voice.

"Yes. Right in front of you, you have one of the immoral people. My full name in Icelandic is Gunnlaugur Sigurðsson."

"It's an ugly name and a long one. But you don't look terrifying," the guest answered, and smiled.

"We're usually what we appear to be, we Icelanders," said George self-importantly.

"But don't you appear rather insignificant when you've dug yourselves down into the hills or into the ice and under the stones?" the traveller asked good-naturedly with a wry smile.

"It's a sheer lie. It's all a thumping lie. I assure you, Mr. Thorndale, that the log cabins and the mud hovels here are no better than the turf houses in Iceland," George answered vehemently.

"I'll believe you, I suppose. I was just saying what I'd heard. Personally I'll believe anything good about you Icelanders, except that you probably have no luck in card games."

The guest was roguish, but George didn't want his last statement to be true of Icelanders.

"I heard about someone many years ago who won a thousand dollars in one night south in St. Louis."

"Do you remember his name?" the visitor asked with great interest.

"Yes. He was Kári's uncle, and his name was Þorsteinn Dal. A great adventurer, but dead now. He was probably killed in the States."

"It's not unlikely that he bit the dust, if he won many nights like the one you tell of," the guest answered seriously, and inadvertently took the silver cross out of the pocket of his dark shirt. He stroked it with his right hand and fingered the flask with his left hand. He must have pulled the cross without thinking, because the silk ribbon around his neck burst. It was held together by a resilient silver lock that appeared to open if it was pulled. The guest quickly closed it and put the cross back into his pocket. George had looked with great interest at the cross, which was eight to ten inches long.

"You must be Catholic if you carry this?" George asked and found that this event gave him the right to find out about the cross.

"No, I'm not," the stranger answered simply. "The cross is a gift from a monk whom I once rescued from the claws of death in a very peculiar way. He also gave me the flask and said that as long as I carried both in the right way, nothing would harm me. He probably meant that I ought never to drink anything stronger than water and that no matter how much I trusted others, I should trust the cross the most."

"Don't you think he rather meant that if you'd nothing better to drink, then it was better to have water than nothing?" said George, who found pure spring water tasteless and not very filling.

"You're probably right: he gave me the flask to use as a last resort. In any case, I like both things and never part with them."

At this point Kári arrived. He was sad and red-eyed from crying. It was as if the strength of youth had left him in one night. When man ceases to believe in himself, he becomes old. Kári suffered not only like the man who throws himself into ruin, but rather like the one who pulls his loved ones with him into the misery and suffers everybody's torments. Now that the hope of saving his mother and brothers and sisters from certain poverty and strained circumstances was gone, and his happy thoughts could no longer ease his workload, his job seemed so hard that he thought he would collapse. It was as if the accumulated fatigue from the time he began in the spring had hidden somewhere in his body and now suddenly crept into his shoulders and weighed him down like a heavy burden.

George introduced Kári to the traveller, who looked at the boy for a long time and greeted him kindly. Then Mr. Thorndale said, "Your friend told me that you'd like to get home as soon as possible and that you've no money. Will you pack your clothes tonight and be ready to come with me early tomorrow morning if I assure you that in a short time you can make money that can be of help to you?"

Kári stared at the traveller with his mouth open. He was greatly surprised, but he liked the guest. This promise from a total stranger gave him, in his desperation, such great hope for good fortune coming his way that it seemed more like the miracle of the guardian spirits in *Arabian Nights* than the cold reality of everyday life. And no matter how it turned out, he felt that he had nothing to lose, however it went, and whatever might happen. The stay here was a torture to him, and to return home seemed impossible. He therefore thanked him for the offer and accepted it without asking a single question: indeed, he had the feeling that he was not supposed to.

Then the traveller asked Kári where he slept, and he showed him.

After that Mr. Thorndale thanked George for the warning and said it might come in handy. But when he had said goodbye to them, he went to the place where he and Jim Dalton had agreed to meet.

George said to Kári that only God knew what the traveller meant by this promise. He had no idea. But he liked the man, even though he might not be what he seemed. The silver cross suggested that the man was either very devout or a completely heathen swindler – but he might well be a good man in either case.

Before the two fellows went to bed, Kári promised George to write and tell him the news when he got to Winnipeg, and George said that he would answer the letter straightaway.

The next morning, well before normal rising time, Mr. Thorndale came to wake up Kári, though it wasn't necessary. Hope and hopelessness struggled so forcefully in his mind that it was impossible for him to sleep at all that night.

After a few minutes they were on their way to the next train station. Kári noticed that his companion's face and hands were scratched. He was certain that the scratches had not been there the night before, but he found it too indiscreet to ask the reason. He did not even know whether or not he and Jim Dalton had been gambling during the night, but he thought it probable in spite of his friend George's warning, and that the changes might stem from that, because he knew that sometimes the fun ended in bloody fistfights and even in fights with weapons, although that was less common.

Kári's travel companion was silent for the first part of the way. But when they had been walking for a while, he started asking Kári about himself, and asked in such great detail about his father, mother, brothers and sisters that Kári was greatly surprised that a stranger should take an interest in such matters.

A short distance from the train station Mr. Thorndale stopped, and he and Kári sat down. "Now I won't be going with you any further, Kári, because my path does not follow this way, although it often crosses it," the traveller said in Icelandic, and Kári looked at him with eyes big with surprise.

"So you're Icelandic!" he exclaimed excitedly.

"At least I once was. I've good news for you – better than the promise I gave you last night. I managed to get your money from Jim Dalton. I say your money, and remember that he was a thief. No gambler, unless he's a thief by nature, has the heart to cheat a sixteen-year-old boy of all he owns in an unfair game. Therefore you need not thank me for the money. It's not mine. The only thing you can thank me for is getting it from the scoundrel."

Then he counted two hundred dollars into Kári's hand, who laughed and cried with joy, but nonetheless refused to take the money, since it was in reality a gift he could not accept.

His travel companion became annoyed. "Are you suggesting that it was right of Jim to cheat you of this money?"

"No, I wouldn't dream of saying that."

"That's what I thought. And if your father had been alive now and seen you betrayed and robbed in this way, wouldn't he have demanded the money from the one who took it?"

"Yes, I imagine he would."

"Then why can't I?"

"Because you're a stranger, and I can't accept money from you without working for it, and since you won it from Jim, it's your profit and not mine."

"All right. You say that you'd have accepted the money if your father had gotten hold of it. Perhaps it's some consolation for you, you little stiffneck, that it's not a stranger who's giving you your money back, but your uncle, Þorsteinn Dal."

Kári was struck dumb with amazement. He hugged his uncle and no longer refused to accept the money. Then he asked his uncle almost shyly, "But why don't you go under your real name, dear uncle?"

"Take it easy, my boy. It's not a different name, if you look at it carefully. At least it's a better translation than your friend Gunnlaugur's, which became George. The first letter in Þorsteinn is clearly the Icelandic *þorn*, and *Thorn* in English, and *dal* is the same as *dale*. But otherwise I never speak about my name or names. There's another thing I want to talk with you about during this short time before we part, because it's unlikely that we'll meet again. Will you promise me firmly and with no exceptions never to gamble? The longing is in the family – is probably in all families – but if it's never practiced, it diminishes until it completely disappears. But those who are once taken in by it for a longer period of time will be at its mercy for the rest of their lives. I know what I'm talking about. Your father once helped me back home in Iceland, more than brothers normally do. I know that he expected nothing in return, but it would be an unspeakable pleasure to me if my sinful soul would rest assured that his son would not become a blot on the national honour like I am, and then I'd feel that I'd paid a part of my debt to him. Therefore I ask you, Kári, in the name of your God, your noble-mindedness, and your nationality, to give me the solemn promise that you never again come near gambling, either in a big or a small way."

"I promise," answered the boy earnestly with tears in his eyes. His uncle took his hand firmly and looked away for a second to hide his feelings. Then he took a small parcel out of his pocket, which he handed to Kári and said, "I ask you to give your mother this parcel along with my greetings. I also ask you and her to remember one thing: I want neither you nor her to mention to anybody that it was me you met. It suits me best to continue being dead in the memory of my countrymen, like I seem to be, and like in fact I am to their society. But some of the people of this country, as for example Jim Dalton, need not know that I'm Icelandic, and for that reason you must not let your friend Gunnlaugur know that I'm anything else but a stranger to you, although I gave you the dollars that Jim took from you in an unfair game. In my view you need not be ashamed that you accepted them from a man who wanted to correct injustice and had previously promised you his help. Gunnlaugur will at least understand this as I think everybody does, except you."

Shortly afterwards they said goodbye. Mr. Thorndale soon disappeared from sight, and Kári continued directly home to his mother in

Winnipeg, and told her the whole story. There was greater joy than words can describe in the small shack, when Kári came home and gave his mother the money, and his brothers and sisters the sweets. And when Gríma opened the parcel from Mr. Thorndale, it turned out that it contained one thousand dollars in gold, silver and bills. Kári's homecoming party turned into a great celebration, and their shack became a secure castle of hope and freedom from cares.

A few days after his return, Kári wrote a letter to George Simpson as he had promised, and related to him all the news he was allowed to tell.

After a few weeks he received the following letter from his friend:

CPR CAMP,
Rocky Mountains

Mr. Kári Árdal
Winnipeg, Manitoba.

Dear friend!
Best greetings. Many blessings.

I've little to report, except to thank you very much for your long letter, full of news. I was sincerely pleased to hear how well your journey went and also that my niece Gunna Sikkhúsdóttir should find such a man as Jói Pálsson of Nes, even though she seemed to have become badly influenced by the English, at least in the eyes of other people. But Gunna is both smart and cute, even though she's my niece.

Here things are as they have always been, as you know. And I'm the same. I'm in good health, and my money-bag keeps getting heavier, thank God. I don't intend to come to Winnipeg before I've saved up a thousand dollars, and God knows when that'll be. But, I tell you, Kári, you were damned lucky to meet such an honest man as this Mr. Thorndale. I always said that. I don't think everybody would have done what he did. But Jimmy says that he's the biggest swindler on two legs on this earth. In fact, there's a story to be told about this. Of course, I only have Jimmy's version of the story. Maybe Mr. Thorndale told you his version, maybe not.

As you recall, I warned Mr. Thorndale many times against playing with such a swindler as Jimmy, and told him your story, which was lucky for you. And he took it all well. Yes, I think he did. And it didn't enter my mind that he'd gamble with him after the long lecture I'd given him. But Jimmy thought that this was some feeble creature, a dilettante and a greenhorn, that could be skinned in a few minutes and would go away silently and cry bitterly, as it's written. But there he was wrong like the old one in days of yore.

Yes, I assure you that Jimmy was furious the morning after you'd gone. Not because you'd left, but because this devil, as he said, had won more than two thousand dollars from him during the night. It may not have been that much, but Jimmy swore that Mr. Thorndale had got his hands on all his money, good and bad: he probably meant both the money he'd won from others and the money he'd worked for, and it must have been no small amount.

And you know what, Kári. It probably turned a bit violent towards the end, because Jimmy was all blue and scratched, and then he says and swears that the silver cross that Mr. Thorndale carries in the silk ribbon was a sheath knife. Can you imagine, Kári? The cross a sheath knife! The upper part of it was the handle, and the lower part was the sheath of the knife, which could be drawn out in a second. But this isn't the end of the story. Not at all. Wonders never cease. That was not all. Jimmy swore to the devil that it was the holy truth that his leather flask, which looked almost more innocent than the cross, was nothing but an artfully created leather case containing two pistols. One only had to press a spring, and it opened, and the revolvers were lying there loaded and handy.

Something must have happened, I assure you, because Mr. Thorndale needed both the cross and the flask, or, rather the knife and the revolver. Jimmy said nothing about their argument, but he said – as he worded it – that it was impossible to trust these travellers, although they appeared to be unarmed and harmless enough, because he said that this fellow had never worked at an honest job, but travelled around gambling like this, for he'd never in his whole life known such a player and such self-control and amazing luck, and he'd known many powerful adventurers in uncle Jonathan's lands.

We here are certain that when Jimmy had lost so much money he tried to hold the knife to his throat and threaten him with violence to return the money, because he naturally considered him unarmed. I tell you, Thorndale quickly showed him the worse side of the cross and the flask.

This letter has gotten longer than most of the letters I've written in my life, except for a few letters I wrote to Iceland when I first got here, but I stopped long ago. So I must end here and ask you to forgive me my poor handwriting. I've nothing to add except that Jimmy deserved this for his treatment of you and others. He's been taken down a peg or two. And I say, as I've always said, that Mr. Thorndale is an honest fellow, no matter what others say.

I hope you're well. And best wishes to you and your family. Farewell.

Your sincere and worthless friend,
George Simpson
(formerly Gunnlaugur Sigurðsson)

Translated by Kirsten Wolf

WHEN THE FOOTPRINTS
BECOME COVERED WITH SNOW

Örn

Örn (pen name for Kristinn Pétursson) was born in 1888 at Neðri Hvesta, Selárdalssókn, in Barðastrandarsýsla. He spent his youth in Arnarfjörður, hence the name Örn. He emigrated to Canada in 1907. No further biographical information about Kristinn Pétursson has come to light.

"When the Footprints Become Covered with Snow" is translated from "Þegar fennir í sporin" in *Heimskringla* 22 December 1926, pp. 2-3. The story was reprinted in Einar H. Kvaran and Guðm. Finnbogason, eds., *Vestan um haf* (Reykjavík, 1930), pp. 533-545.

NATURE BOASTS of many strange things, and yet man is the strangest of all.

It never even entered my mind that there could be two sides to Svend Knutson, yet so it turned out to be. It was only by chance – something that happened to Svend himself – that I got to see him and know him the way he used to be. And perhaps he is still the same, because I think there are few who have seen behind the threshold of his soul.

I was a newcomer, and, as you know, there were usually two things I and my fellow countrymen could choose to work at – either the ditches in Winnipeg or the roads – and I chose the latter. A few hundred miles east of Winnipeg a railway was being laid; the track was hewn out of the iron-hard rock. This railway now stretches from coast to coast.

I had little experience in clearing stone. I was young and not yet of full strength, and I readily admit that I was not worth much those first days I worked there.

It was there I first saw Svend Knutson. He was a foreman over a large number of men, mostly Swedes and Norwegians, who were the greatest workhorses.

Svend was about six feet tall and very burly, blond and blue-eyed. His eyes were quite beautiful, when you could see them, but that was not always possible. It was as if the eyelids, both upper and lower, lay in indelible wrinkles and folds, and although his eyes were in reality big, they would appear small to most people. His forehead was of average height, but wide and round; his brows were shaggy and thick with deep furrows between them. He had a long and thick moustache, so that his mouth was mostly hidden. His chin was wide and strong and protruded somewhat.

I doubt that anyone who met him on the road, even his associates, would have considered him to be of a delicate constitution, because it was impossible to see anything delicate about his physical appearance. Yet it was the voice I found to be the most formidable about the man, and then his hands; they were not particularly large, but the joints were extremely thick, and the backs of the hands were hairy down to the fingers.

He left me mostly alone for the first two days I worked, only telling me what to do. And of course, the job was not difficult for those who were used to it; but for me it was drudgery, even though I understood what needed to be done. It does not take much skill to push a wheelbarrow filled with rocks.

It was then my third day there, close to noon. The day was hot and sultry and made the sweat pour down my face. The clothes stuck to my body. The wheelbarrow had slid off the planks on which I was to drive, and this was the third time in a row that this had happened. I was having difficulty getting the wheelbarrow up onto the planks again.

"Get out of the way!" someone bellowed in Norwegian right behind me. It was Svend. Then he grabbed the wheelbarrow full of rocks and pulled it forcefully onto the planks, rolled it where the rocks were to go, brought it back empty, and threw it at me.

"How in the name of the devil can railways be built, if they're to be built by men like you? I don't see how in hell you can slide the wheelbarrow off the planks; an eighty-year-old hag with a broken ass could do the job better than you."

He spoke so loudly that every man who was near must have heard him.

130

I will not attempt to explain how angry I was. With all my might and main, I had been trying to do my best, and that devil of a man must have been able to see and understand that. But what could I do? I did not have enough command of the Norwegian language to be able to answer back. I understood very little English, and I had no mind to run away like a beaten dog; of course, it was no easy matter, through woods and bogs, and I didn't know the way. So I shrugged and took the wheelbarrow silently.

I have to admit, however, that those were the only insulting words he spoke to me all summer, while the job lasted. In the afternoon that same day, he gave me another job to do that was easier.

Nonetheless, the longer we worked together, the closer I felt to him. And I was not the only one who got into trouble with him. I soon heard that he was wont to give others a severe tongue-lashing when he thought it necessary, just as he had given me that time.

Svend was not talkative at work or elsewhere; nevertheless, he could sometimes be amusing. I think he spoke with me more than any of the others, especially if we were alone.

And slowly but surely he looked less like a troll and more like a man in my eyes. But I found out from others, especially those who knew him best, that he was known to drink more than a little. . . .

We came to Winnipeg late that autumn. The job that Knutson had overseen was finished, and some of the men who had worked with him travelled with him, including myself. Many took jobs here and there on the railway.

Knutson spoke about settling on his farm, which was close to Winnipeg, over the winter.

But the rest of us intended to get jobs, wherever we received the best offers.

Svend and some of his men felt the need to take some refreshment the day we arrived. I did not really belong with the group and took a room in a boarding house on the outskirts of the town.

Three days later I had secured a fishing job on Lake Winnipeg and was leaving the next day. Then, to my surprise, I met Svend.

I was walking downtown, not thinking about anything, when all of a sudden I saw Svend standing and staring south down the street. He did not answer when I greeted him. I stopped and looked in the same direction. I thought that perhaps there had been an accident, but

I saw nothing except a crowd of people moving back and forth.

"What are you looking at, Svend?" I finally asked, when I saw nothing out of the ordinary.

"You here!" he said, when he finally noticed that I was standing beside him.

He stood silently a while longer looking in the same direction; then he quickly turned towards me. I had the feeling that a man was speaking in his sleep, when he said, "Come with me, Gunnar; I have to talk with you."

We walked silently over to the hotel where he was staying. He pulled out a chair in the room where he slept, or was supposed to sleep, at night. To me it looked as if he had not slept much that night.

"Sit down," he said. I did. For a few minutes he paced up and down the room, hunched over with his hands behind his back. I was about to address him, when he stopped and straightened himself and beat his fists together, so that the room resounded, "What a damnable devil of a dog I am! Here I've been lying like a pig for three days since we came in. It's been three days, hasn't it?"

"Almost four," I said.

"Yes, quite right, four." Then he threw himself into a chair beside me. "And then of all days I had to meet her now; right now, the way I look!"

"Was it your wife you were staring after, when I bumped into you just now?"

"No, it wasn't my wife. I wouldn't have minded so much, if I'd met my wife. I only hope that she wouldn't have recognized me." He said it as if he was talking to himself.

"But who was this woman?" I asked.

"That's exactly what I want to tell you about. I'm a bloody fool to be blabbering about what is long past and most often forgotten by myself. It's likely the damned alcohol that makes me so tender-hearted. I've never told anyone this before; but now I feel I must tell someone about this little adventure, and you're the man I'd rather tell it to than any other. Perhaps it's because I think we won't meet again, and even if you laugh at me it doesn't matter, because I won't know.

"I was about seventeen years old, when I saw her for the first time. She was then a maidservant in a home where I lived. She was tall and slim, and carried herself like a queen. Her hair was long and golden. Her face was rather long, but well-proportioned. I'll not try to describe her further; I'll only say that she was the most beautiful girl I've ever seen before or since.

"The farm had double occupancy as long as my mother lived; but when she died, which was two years before this happened, my father gave up his household and worked for his brother, who had worked half the farm opposite my father. Then my uncle took over the whole farm.

"Andrés was the name of my uncle's son. He was one year older than I, mature and courageous in all he did. I, on the other hand, was slow to mature and smaller than average for my age.

"I remember how it grieved me, when Jóhanna – that was the girl's name – stood on tiptoes beside me, held up her arms and smiled, as if to say, 'Come here, you poor devil and stand under my armpit; you're so small, poor baby.' And it didn't take her long to see that I disliked this behaviour, because if I was slow to act or pretended that I didn't want to do what she asked me to do, then her usual comment was, 'Svend, should I measure you?' She really didn't have to threaten me, to turn me around in circles and use me like a shepherd boy; I'd have paid a great deal of money for the pleasure that came with the privilege of being her slave. I certainly would have felt heartbroken if she'd never asked anything of me.

"'But how were things between her and Andrés?' I asked. Then Svend smiled, and I could not decide whether it was a mournful smile or a sardonic grin.

"There everything was reversed. It was she who revolved around Andrés, and it was usually when I was reluctant to do what she asked of me that I knew I was really doing it for Andrés. But when it was thus she never teased me, and when she saw that I hesitated, then her usual comment was, 'Svenni, you do it for me.' Andrés! How I hated him when he teased and mocked her to no end. Those were my unhappiest times – when I saw that she was hurt – and it happened rather often. She usually walked quietly away and held her head high; and it was always forgotten after a few minutes, even when Andrés had managed to make her angry.

"One day I remember particularly well. I came running into a room that was used for storage. Jóhanna stood there and was doing – or pretended to be doing – some laundry. She had her back to me when I came in, but I saw that she was crying. I stood there as if I were nailed to the ground. The errand was forgotten.

"All I knew was that she was crying. And before I realized what I was doing, I was by her side and had my hands around her neck; I put my head up against her cheek and cried too, unable to utter even one word.

"She was combing my hair with her fingers, when I came to my senses.

"'Is Andrés to blame for this?' I groaned.

"'No, my dear Svenni. Why do you say that? Just some nonsense I was thinking about. And you started to cry too,' she said and laughed aloud. 'What a terrible baby you are.' Then she pushed me away, both gently and playfully. 'Come now, run outside and dry your tears.'

"A year and a half passed without any great events taking place. It was late in the autumn. Andrés had left a while ago to study at an agricultural college, and I was gradually maturing physically. The relationship between myself and Jóhanna was the same as before: kind playfulness from her side and silent adoration from mine. I think that no prisoner has rejoiced in his freedom more than I rejoiced in the arrival of winter. Andrés was now gone, and I anticipated that our lives, Jóhanna's and mine, would become more entwined than before. To be sure, there were others in the home, but they were like half-forgotten human beings in another land; they had not much to do with our lives.

"But then suddenly a cloud appeared in my blissful heaven. The summer chores were all finished, and the winter chores were not so great that the whole family would have much to do, so Jóhanna took the opportunity and asked her mistress's permission to visit her relatives, who lived in the neighbouring valley. It was granted, and Jóhanna prepared for the trip. I didn't like the news; yet I reassured myself that the two or, at the most, three weeks were bound to pass somehow.

"The landscape was such that the fjord where I lived and the fjord where Jóhanna's relatives lived cut into the land on a slant from each other. In this way they formed a fairly wide peninsula, which became narrower the further inland the fjords came. Into this peninsula long and narrow valleys were carved, guarded by mountains on three sides.

"The stipulation for Jóhanna's leave of absence was that she get herself a guide over the mountains, and as I wished and hoped for, she came to me first.

"We left early in the morning and walked into the valley as the route lay, because it was impossible to get up from the floor of the valley on horseback. The journey in the valley was quick; we broke into a run occasionally and walked slowly in between and chatted about everything. At the end of the valley floor the hills rose in succession. We climbed the hills briskly, and before we knew it, we stood at the base of the highest and most gigantic hill. We agreed to rest for a short while before we tackled it, and sat down side by side.

"'I don't know how I'd have made it, if you hadn't been so kind as to escort me.'

"'Oh, you'd have managed to get someone else to escort you,' I said.

"'Well, I don't know if anyone else would have done it, even if I'd asked them, at least not without some discussion. And I preferred to have you with me, Svend.'

"'Rather than Andrés, if he'd been here?'

"It was not without effort that I asked that question, and I don't know why I asked; perhaps hidden resentment towards Andrés stirred within me, perhaps towards both of them. I saw that she blushed.

"'Yes, rather than Andrés,' she answered after a short deliberation. 'But why do you ask, boy? I wasn't thinking about Andrés. Do you perhaps regret that you promised to escort me?'

"'Oh no, far from it. And I wouldn't want you to get lost or to get caught by the kelpie, which lives in the lakes in the other valley. It's said that it can be dangerous for young and beautiful girls to travel alone along the shores of the lakes,' I said, and laughed.

"She laughed too.

"'Let's keep on going.'

"We proceeded speedily up to the edge, but there it was so steep that it was hardly possible to obtain a firm foothold on the scree, and in some places there were small snowdrifts left from the previous winter. It was in one of these drifts that Jóhanna almost lost her foothold. I caught her hand when she slipped. After that I held her hand with my right one, but used the left one to grab onto things where the slope was the steepest. Thus we felt our way up over the edge.

"The peak of the mountain was only a few hundred yards wide. We walked in silence to the edge of the other valley, still holding hands.

"The valley that now lay beneath us looked different from the one we had left behind. Low belts of crags, with screes in some places that stretched up onto the edge, sealed the valley from above. Beneath it a long and almost levelled plane started, with small lakes and wooded areas here and there, and further down the valley the plane ended in two or three steep slopes; there by the sea stood the farmhouse where Jóhanna's relatives lived. It had snowed a little in the valley, but the snow had been blown away up on the edge. And there the valley lay beneath, all white with the small dark lakes hither and thither, and bits of woodland that had shaken off the snow.

"'Wait here while I find a good place to get down,' I said.

"She let go of my hand rather slowly.

"'For God's sake, be careful! I don't want to be the cause of your death, or I'd also want to go with you.' And now there was no smile on her face.

"I ran light as a lamb along the edge, until I found a pass where it was easy to go down. I called that she should come, and ran towards her.

"'Let's hold hands,' she said, when we met, and extended her hand to me. It was just what I had hoped for. I took her hand in silence, and thus we went down into the valley hand-in-hand. Neither one of us said much. It seemed that we had only gone a short distance when I realized that we were already down by the lower slope, and there not so far beneath us the farmhouse of Jóhanna's relatives lay before our eyes. Jóhanna stopped.

"'You have escorted me much further than you should have. You must have the light of day to get over the ridge, if not farther, because it is so difficult to find one's way there, even though I naturally know that you are not afraid of a kelpie or of the dark,' she said and smiled a little.

"I protested. I wanted to escort her further, but it was not to be discussed. She said that I was expected home that evening; otherwise I could have stayed overnight at her relatives.

"'And therefore we must say goodbye,' she said and extended her hand to me.

"'Farewell and bless you. I don't know how or when I can repay you for escorting me.'

"I looked into her eyes. I knew very well how she could repay me – and repay me again and again. Just one kiss. I have never wished for anything so passionately nor longed so greatly for anything as for that kiss from her. And I don't know what or how any power could have held me back from uttering that wish.

"Was it my own arrogance that held me back from asking for what I felt was mine by right? Or is there somewhere some unknown power that weaves our fate without our consent and regardless of our wishes or hopes. Maybe. Just one kiss in itself is a trifle, but nevertheless, it can give rise to great events. Just one kiss could have completely changed our lives.

"And thus we parted.

"I stood and watched her go, until she disappeared beneath the edge of the slope. Could it be that she wouldn't look back? No, she didn't.

"I turned my face towards home. The way was not hard to find; our footprints in the snow showed me the way. I walked beside the trail without stepping on it anywhere; to disturb the footprints was to me a sacrilege. But now it started to snow. It snowed off and on, and a light gust of wind blew the snowflakes to and fro. As the footprints became fainter and fainter, I looked on them with sorrow. I walked as fast as I possibly could on the side where her footprints lay. I ran. I wanted to follow them as far as possible before they disappeared for good.

"Another gust of wind and one more snow shower! I could hardly see the trail. I hoped to see it better when it cleared up. It cleared up. I was nearing the edge of the valley and saw the pass where we had come down. I stood in the place where I knew we had walked. The footprints certainly didn't exist any more.

"I looked back and saw a small spot of the fjord and the farthest point of land on the other side. I saw the foam of the surf rush into the air and make a white fringe along the shore. And it seemed to me that I felt the waves of the future break on the sands of my soul and carve their runes there. Never, never will your lives entwine again. And your footprints have disappeared for eternity.

"I threw myself down into the snow and cried like a baby, bitterly and painfully. But by and by I heard another voice, mild and soft: 'Your footprints were pure like the snow that covered them. And the memory lives unscathed.'

"I hurried home. Jóhanna stayed on with her relatives. The following summer I went to America. I sometimes wrote to my father, but I avoided asking about Jóhanna; and he hardly mentioned her except to say that she had moved away somewhere. Three years passed. I thought about her often and about our footprints in the snow. And I tried to keep my life pure like those memories.

"I don't know what I wanted. Yet I think I must have been hoping that we would meet again, some time or another. And I always saw her as she was when we parted at home in the valley.

"And then I saw her one day. It was at a gathering of Swedes and Norwegians in the summer that I met her and a man who was with her. I recognized her instantly and she me. She was even more beautiful than before. Now she was a grown woman. But there was something in her face I didn't recognize. Was it the mark of loss or of gain? I didn't know.

"'Well, well, as I live and breathe, it's Svend! My, what a great and dangerously huge fellow you have become!'

"Then she stood on her tiptoes, stretched out her arm and smiled like she had done so often before. I heartily wished good fortune to her and her future husband.

"Many years have passed since. I've a wife and children and love them as much as the next man does his. But you understand, I've changed a lot, and my footprints are not pure anymore, at least not all of them, even though I have rarely stepped down so hard that they have not soon been covered over. But then perhaps it's not so important what others see of our lives. It's probably more important what we know about ourselves.

"Jóhanna is also changed. I see her sometimes, mostly from afar. I don't know if she recognizes me now. She's all right, or so I believe.

She has many promising children. But wrinkles have started to show on her face and white strands in her golden hair. And it is like a stab to my own body, each additional wrinkle and each strand of hair I see turn grey. I only hope that she didn't recognize me just now."

Svend stood up.

"I go home today. Farewell," he said, and extended his hand to me.

I've not been able to forget Svend, or his story. Perhaps it reminds me of old footprints that deserve to remain pure.

Translated by Árný Hjaltadóttir